The French Rococo

GREAT ARTISTS OF THE WESTERN WORLD

The French Rococo

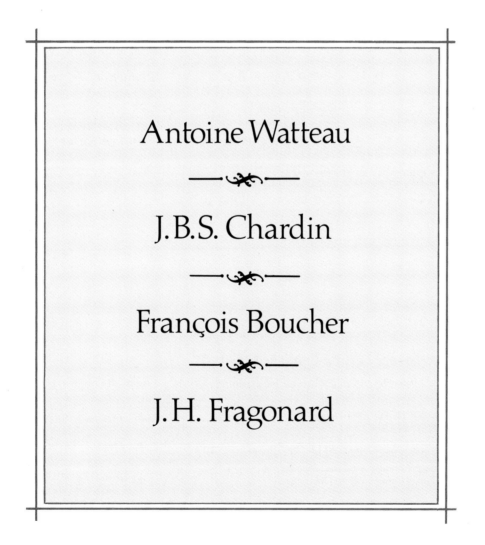

Antoine Watteau

J.B.S. Chardin

François Boucher

J.H. Fragonard

MARSHALL CAVENDISH · LONDON · NEW YORK · SYDNEY

Staff Credits

Editors	Clive Gregory LL B Sue Lyon BA (Honours)	**Picture Researchers**	Vanessa Fletcher BA (Honours) Flavia Howard BA (Honours) Jessica Johnson BA
Art Editors	Kate Sprawson BA (Honours) Keith Vollans LSIAD		
Deputy Editor	John Kirkwood B Sc (Honours)	**Production Controllers**	Steve Roberts Alan Stewart BSc
Sub-editors	Caroline Bugler BA (Honours), MA Sue Churchill BA (Honours) Alison Cole BA, M Phil Jenny Mohammadi Nigel Rodgers BA (Honours), MA Penny Smith Will Steeds BA (Honours), MA	**Secretary**	Lynn Smail
		Publisher	Terry Waters Grad IOP
		Editorial Director	Maggi McCormick
		Production Executive	Robert Paulley B Sc
		Consultant and Authenticator	Sharon Fermor BA (Honours) Lecturer in the Extra-Mural Department of London University and Lecturer in Art History at Sussex University
Designers	Stuart John Julie Stanniland		

Reference Edition Published 1990

Published by Marshall Cavendish Corporation
147 West Merrick Road
Freeport, Long Island
N.Y. 11520

Typeset by Litho Link Ltd., Welshpool
Printed and Bound in Singapore by
Times Offset Private Ltd.

Library of Congress Cataloging-in-Publication Data

Main entry under title:

Great Artists of the Western World.

Includes index.
1. Artists – Biography. I. Marshall Cavendish Corporation
N40.G77 1987   709'.2'2 [B]   86–23863
ISBN 0–86307–743–9

ISBN 0–86307–743–9 (set)
       0–86307–748–X (vol)

Preface

Looking at pictures can be one of the greatest pleasures that life has to offer. Note, however, those two words 'can be'; all too many of us remember all too clearly those grim afternoons of childhood when we were dragged, bored to tears and complaining bitterly, through room after room of Italian primitives by well-meaning relations or tight-lipped teachers. It was enough to put one off pictures for life – which, for some of us, was exactly what it did.

For if gallery-going is to be the fun it should be, certain conditions must be fulfilled. First, the pictures we are to see must be good pictures. Not necessarily great pictures – even a few of these can be daunting, while too many at a time may prove dangerously indigestible. But they must be well-painted, by good artists who know precisely both the effect they want to achieve and how best to achieve it. Second, we must limit ourselves as to quantity. Three rooms – four at the most – of the average gallery are more than enough for one day, and for best results we should always leave while we are still fresh, well before satiety sets in. Now I am well aware that this is a counsel of perfection: sometimes, in the case of a visiting exhibition or, perhaps, when we are in a foreign city with only a day to spare, we shall have no choice but to grit our teeth and stagger on to the end. But we shall not enjoy ourselves quite so much, nor will the pictures remain so long or so clearly in our memory.

The third condition is all-important: we must know something about the painters whose work we are looking at. And this is where this magnificent series of volumes – one of which you now hold in your hands – can make all the difference. No painting is an island: it must, if it is to be worth a moment's attention, express something of the personality of its painter. And that painter, however individual a genius, cannot but reflect the country, style and period, together with the views and attitudes of the people among whom he or she was born and bred. Even a superficial understanding of these things will illuminate a painting for us far better than any number of spotlights, and if in addition we have learnt something about the artist as a person – life and loves, character and beliefs, friends and patrons, and the places to which he or she travelled – the interest and pleasure that the work will give us will be multiplied a hundredfold.

Great Artists of the Western World will provide you with just such an insight into the life and work of some of the outstanding painters of Europe and America. The text is informative without ever becoming dry or academic, not limiting itself to the usual potted biographies but forever branching out into the contemporary world outside and beyond workshop or studio. The illustrations, in colour throughout, have been dispensed in almost reckless profusion. For those who, like me, revel in playing the Attribution Game – the object of which is to guess the painter of each picture before allowing one's eye to drop to the label – the little sections on 'Trademarks' are a particularly happy feature; but every aficionado will have particular preferences, and I doubt whether there is an art historian alive, however distinguished, who would not find some fascinating nugget of previously unknown information among the pages that follow.

This series, however, is not intended for art historians. It is designed for ordinary people like you and me – and for our older children – who are fully aware that the art galleries of the world constitute a virtually bottomless mine of potential enjoyment, and who are determined to extract as much benefit and advantage from it as they possibly can. All the volumes in this collection will enable us to do just that, expanding our knowledge not only of art itself but also of history, religion, mythology, philosophy, fashion, interior decoration, social customs and a thousand other subjects as well. So let us not simply leave them around, flipping idly through a few of their pages once in a while. Let us read them as they deserve to be read – and welcome a new dimension in our lives.

John Julius Norwich is a writer and broadcaster who has written histories of Venice and of Norman Sicily as well as several works on history, art and architecture. He has also made over twenty documentary films for television, including the recent **Treasure Houses of Britain** *series which was widely acclaimed after repeated showings in the United States.*

Lord Norwich is Chairman of the Venice in Peril Fund, and member of the Executive Committee of the British National Trust, an independently funded body established for the protection of places of historic interest and natural beauty.

John Julius Norwich

Contents

Introduction

The feature which unites the painters involved in the Rococo movement is their desire to make nature the foundation of their art. This may seem surprising to the modern spectator, for whom the style probably conjures up a fantasy world, peopled with rosy-cheeked cherubs, sprightly young goddesses and lovers idling away their time in theatrical costume. Indeed, such impressions are not wholly incorrect – for it was a selective brand of naturalism that the Rococo painters espoused – but they should be viewed against the alternative art forms that were currently available.

The Rococo style developed as a reaction against the pomp and solemnity of Baroque and Classical painting. In part, this was due to the decline of the latter – French history painting lost much of its impetus after the death of Poussin – but it also marked a distinct shift in the patterns of patronage. The death of Louis XIV in 1715 signalled the end of an era. The Court returned to Paris from its majestic isolation at Versailles and sparked off a boom in the building trade, as a wealth of town houses or hôtels appeared in the capital. These new residences required a more intimate form of decoration than that employed in the great palaces.

Alongside these commissions from the nobility, there was also a growing market provided by the more prosperous ranks of the bourgeoisie. And these bourgeois patrons gave their protégés a comparatively free hand in their painting.

A Restless Spirit
This freedom was particularly crucial to Watteau. His attempt to produce a history painting for the Prix de Rome ended in failure and he was extremely fortunate in gaining the Academy's permission to choose his own subject for his 'reception piece'. Even a successful candidate like Boucher, when winning the Prix de Rome in 1723, had to produce a painting on the unwieldy theme of 'Evilmerodach, son and successor of Nebuchadnezzar, delivering Joachim from the chains in which he had long been held by his father'. Little wonder then that the major artists of the period developed outside the suffocating spheres of the Academy.

Of the four painters covered in this volume, Watteau was the most rebellious. His art, like his lifestyle, was constantly changing but, in common with other Rococo painters, the most frequent accusation to be levelled against Watteau was that his art was escapist. For the Revolutionary generation, his work epitomized the indolent fantasies of the Ancien Régime, while other, more recent, commentators have preferred to view his

The artists
(from left to right) a pastel portrait of Watteau by Rosalba Carriera; a probable self-portrait of Fragonard, dressed in all his finery as a young man; Chardin's simple but direct Self-portrait with Eye-shade *shows the artist in his mid-seventies; a pastel portrait of Boucher, aged about 40, by Gustav Lundberg.*

Giraudon

Museo Civico, Trevise

Musée Fragonard, Grasse

Giraudon/Collection of M. Arthur Veil-Picard

outdoor idylls as a retreat from the squalor and suffering of ill-health. Neither paints a complete picture, however, for Watteau's art was firmly rooted in naturalism.

At the core of Watteau's achievement was his superb draughtsmanship. He had sketched from his earliest years in Valenciennes, and in his brief life amassed several large volumes of chalk drawings. These were usually made for Watteau's own enjoyment – unlike most artists, he rarely made formal studies for a composition – and are probably a reflection of his impatience, since a drawn image could be captured far more quickly than a painted one. Watteau preferred to depict the people he saw around him – beggars, street musicians, soldiers, actors, clowns – rather than rely on models in a studio, and there is no doubt that his paintings grew out of his sketches. His first real success, for example, came from the military scenes which he

painted at the border town of Valenciennes in 1709.

These military scenes, which were in effect compilations of individual figure drawings, can seem anecdotal and fragmented. However, when Watteau applied the same technique to the actors he observed in Paris, it conveyed an entirely different impression, one of ambiguity and suggestiveness. His players' glances and gestures hinted at the minutiae of love as it blossoms or fades.

Watteau did not exhaust this theme. In his last great painting, the L'Enseigne de Gersaint (pp.34-5), he took his characters indoors and clothed them in modern dress, but retained the subtle interplay of relationships between the figures. It was, in many ways, Watteau's most successful blend of naturalism and theatricality and its evident signs of a new departure in his work make his premature demise all the more tragic.

A Master of Sensuality

Boucher had much in common with Watteau. Both men complemented their excellent draughtsmanship with a taste for the rich colouring of Rubens and the Venetian school. Like Watteau, Boucher's affection for the theatre was profoundly influential. From 1737, he designed scenery for the Paris Opéra, and this experience had a telling effect on his work in other media, from the tapestries to the interior decorations, causing him to concentrate his energies on the foreground and the full width of the picture-space. This is particularly noticeable in Boucher's landscapes.

Boucher could rival Watteau's technical skill, but he lacked his flair for invention. As a result, he was generally content to supply the artistic

Fragonard's flamboyant style
(centre) Fragonard frequently altered his style to suit his subject-matter – as in this painting, Rinaldo in the Gardens of Armida. The painting is executed in quick, sketchy brush-strokes which create a feeling of restlessness, and the dramatic effect is intensified by 'spotlighting' the two main figures.

demands of the new breed of moneyed patrons. What the latter wanted was essentially a domestic version of history painting. Mythological themes were still popular, provided they dispensed with the moral or heroic implications of their subject and dwelt instead on the purely decorative aspects.

The pre-eminence of decoration was the most important feature of the Rococo style and its spirit pervaded every branch of the arts, from architecture to furniture. Outside painting, it was characterized by a number of readily identifiable forms. These included rocaille (a delicate rock and plant motif that gave its name to the style), leaf and scrollwork, luscious arrangements of curves and chinoiserie designs. Painters, clearly, could not incorporate these into their pictures, but there was a tendency to introduce small, precious objects or rich materials into their compositions.

The Artist of the Boudoir
Rococo was also very much the art of the boudoir. The theme of love was a common thread running through the work of Watteau and Boucher, reaching its climax in the paintings of Fragonard. In his youth, Fragonard trained under both Chardin and Boucher, but evidently felt a greater affinity with the latter. His scenes of amorous dalliance seemed to carry on where Boucher's left off, save that Fragonard no longer felt the need to use any pictorial pretexts. His lovers were not actors or goddesses, but the people of his own time.

Rapidly, Fragonard evolved a style to suit his subject matter. Like his predecessors, he preferred to deal with flirtation and seduction rather than passion and his approach was correspondingly nimble. Everything in his pictures seems as insubstantial as a lover's whispered promises. The light flickers erratically, spotlighting the main characters, and nature acts as an accomplice in the lovers' play. Luxuriant, frothy boughs of trees, rumpled folds of silk, or rising clouds of steam surround the figures and mask their actions with a suggestive air.

Fragonard's paintings reflected the prevailing attitudes of his time. In literature, the solemn, moral dramas of Racine and Corneille had been superseded by the writings of Marivaux and Laclos, where the problems of love were dissected with an elegant lightness of touch. Their frankness was echoed in real life by Louis XV, who openly paraded his mistress, Madame de Pompadour, at Court.

A Painter of Quiet Dignity
Inevitably, a reaction was bound to come. From the 1740s, Diderot and his fellow philosophes began to rail against the artificiality and the licentiousness of painters like Boucher and Fragonard. In their place, Diderot advocated the work of Chardin and Greuze, warmly praising their truth to nature and their appreciation of domestic virtue. Certainly, there was a world of difference between the art of Chardin and that of his pupil, Fragonard. Where the latter was a virtuoso, working at a breakneck pace, Chardin was slow and meticulous. Where Fragonard, even in his genre scenes, stressed the sensual aspect of his theme, Chardin sought only to describe his subjects with clinical accuracy.

In part, the direction of Chardin's art may be accounted for by his lack of formal training. An Academy education might well have prompted him to emulate the more stately still-life painting of Oudry or Desportes (p.46). However, his genre scenes demonstrated the unbridgeable gulf that separated him from the Rococo painters. His Saying Grace (p.63) was painted at almost the same time as Boucher's Le Déjeuner (p.90), but the treatment was radically different. Ignoring the class distinctions that are apparent in the two households, it is still noticeable that Boucher delighted most in depicting the casual folds of his materials, the graceful fall of light from the window and an agreeable sense of clutter. Chardin, in contrast, stripped away most unnecessary detail and imbued the remaining objects with far greater solidity. His palette was subdued and his treatment of the light and the draperies was ordered and regular. (Chardin rarely included windows in his interiors. His rooms just melt away into shadow.) In tone, his work exuded gravity, where Boucher's exhibited an air of pleasure. In this sense, it has been argued that Chardin brought to still-life and genre painting a new, quiet dignity.

In due course, however, Chardin's fortunes waned along with those of the Rococo painters. By 1773, the growing Neo-Classical movement had advanced sufficiently for Madame du Barry to reject Fragonard's superb Pursuit of Love series as old-fashioned, and the Revolution left him and Greuze isolated as relics of a bygone age. Not until the Goncourt brothers produced their influential survey, in the mid-19th century, did the Rococo style regain its reputation as a major tradition in European art.

ant Watteau

1684-1721

Antoine Watteau was the most important French painter of the 18th century, helping to shape the development of the Rococo style. His tragically short life bears all the hallmarks of romantic fiction. Of humble provincial origins, Watteau was the child of a brutish father. He arrived in Paris destitute, but by good luck he found work with the decorative artists Claude Gillot and Claude III Audran.

These teachers aided Watteau in the creation of the *fêtes galantes* – theatrical idylls where costumed figures stroll in wooded parklands – which are the artist's most distinctive achievement. He brought to this genre a gift for magical colouring and imbued such works with an air of gentle melancholy. Watteau died from tuberculosis at the age of 37, just as his style was entering a new phase of naturalistic grandeur.

A Restless Spirit

Introspective, withdrawn and prone to self-criticism, Watteau spent his relatively brief life in continual movement between the houses of his fiercely devoted friends and patrons.

Antoine Watteau was born in October 1684, in the border town of Valenciennes. Although this town had been ceded from the Spanish Netherlands to France by the Treaty of Nijmegen six years earlier, Watteau's contemporaries always thought of him as a Flemish painter.

The artist's father, a master tiler and carpenter, was a colourful character with a reputation for drunkenness and brawling but he appears to have had some sympathy with his son's artistic leanings for, at the age of about eleven, the young Watteau was apprenticed to a local painter, possibly Jacques-Albert Gérin. But the devotional works which the latter produced for nearby churches do not seem to have inspired young Antoine and, by 1702, the apprenticeship seems to have ended, for reasons which have always remained unclear.

Watteau swiftly attached himself to a new master, an obscure theatrical scene-painter whose name has not been documented. Together, they went to Paris, where Watteau's teacher had occasionally been employed at the Opéra. Almost immediately, however, the artist abandoned his youthful charge and returned to Valenciennes. Penniless and without friends, Watteau resorted to the most menial of artistic tasks, turning out cheap painted copies of portraits and saints. For this, he joined an assembly line of workers, each of whom executed a small section of the picture – the sky, the drapery or the faces – before passing it on to one of his colleagues.

Fortunately, Watteau's talents were not constrained for long with this demeaning labour. By 1703, he had made the acquaintance of Claude Gillot, who employed him as an assistant. Gillot's best work was as a draughtsman and illustrator, but his true value to Watteau lay in the introduction he gave him to the world of the theatre. In particular, Gillot took Watteau to the

Border birthplace
(below) Watteau's home town of Valenciennes is in northern France close to the Belgian frontier. Valenciennes had been taken from the occupying Spaniards by a French army under Louis XIV.

Theatrical inspiration
(right) It is not hard to see why the young Watteau, newly arrived in Paris, was enraptured with things theatrical. At the time, the lavishness and opulence of stage productions were truly magnificent.

A feast of entertainment
(left) Claude Gillot, Watteau's mentor in his early years in Paris, often took him to country fairs around the city. These could be the entertainments of the wealthy – here, a party is being given by the Prince of Conti – or the simple celebrations of everyday folk. At these events there would often be an impromptu performance of Italian Comedy, the sophistication of which would be dictated by the wealth of the sponsors. Watteau fell in love with these performances and culled countless images from them.

Ollivier; Fête donnée par le Prince de Conti a l'Isle Adam/Versailles

Key Dates

1684 born in the French border town of Valenciennes

1702 goes to Paris

c.1703-07 employed by Claude Gillot as his pupil and assistant

c.1707-08 working for the decorative artist, Claude Audran

1709 fails to win the Prix de Rome. Returns briefly to Valenciennes and paints military scenes

1712 granted associate membership of the Academy

1717 *Pilgrimage to the Island of Cythera* finally presented to the Academy

1718 lodges with Vleughels

1719 travels to London to consult Dr Mead about his failing health

1720 returns to Paris and stays with Gersaint

1721 resides at Nogent where he dies in Gersaint's arms

Rococo teacher
(above) Claude Audran had a great influence on Watteau who worked with him for a short while.

Spring
(below) This charming picture shows Watteau's genius in full bloom. It is one of a set of four seasons commissioned by Pierre Crozat.

Parisian fairs, where the boy witnessed the improvised performances of the Italian Comedy. At the time, these were played by French actors, since a satirical reference to one of Louis XIV's mistresses had resulted in the banishment of the Italians. However, Gillot had been in Paris before the ban and conveyed his enthusiasm for their fresh, inventive style to his eager protégé. Soon, Watteau was outdoing his master's rather prosaic theatrical scenes, creating from this subject-matter a new category of painting, the *fête galante*.

A DIFFICULT PERSONALITY

Watteau's association with Gillot ended in 1707, when the two men quarrelled. One strand, in fact, runs throughout Watteau's life: his 'difficult' personality; all Watteau's friends commented on his awkward temperament. He was irritable, restless and withdrawn. Flattery made him impatient and with strangers he was usually distant. He was also uninterested in money; a colleague related how Watteau once gave a wig-maker two pictures in exchange for a wig and still felt apprehensive, lest the man might feel he had been underpaid.

In some measure, Watteau's moody nature may be attributed to the serious illness – tuberculosis – which afflicted him for most of his career and which was eventually to cut it short. It is open to speculation as to how early the disease was apparent to Watteau, but it is frequently assumed that it 'infected' his paintings with the air of melancholy surrounding his costumed figures, casting a shadow over their festivities.

Nonetheless, Watteau's friends were rarely alienated by his unpredictable behaviour. Gillot, for example, recommended Watteau to his next master, Claude III Audran, one of the founding

Pannini; Concert Scene/Louvre, Paris

Fotomas

Sirois and his Family
(left) One of Watteau's good friends was the art dealer Sirois with whom Watteau stayed from time to time in Paris. Sirois was the father-in-law to another art dealer called Edme Gersaint for whom Watteau painted the famous L'Enseigne de Gersaint, *a shop sign for his picture gallery. The depiction of Sirois as a theatrical player shows the broadness of handling that indicates Watteau's mature period.*

clear demand for more. Valenciennes, as a border town, was the ideal place for the artist to build up a stock of drawings depicting soldiers on the march or resting in their camps.

By 1710, however, Watteau was back in Paris, taking with him his pupil, Jean-Baptiste Pater. Watteau lodged with the art dealer Sirois for the next two years and it may have been through his shop that he came into contact with the wealthy collector, Pierre Crozat. Watteau stayed intermittently with the latter between 1712 and 1715, visiting his country house near Enghien. It was a mark of Crozat's hospitality that he managed to persuade Watteau to undertake one of his few specific commissions, a series of *Seasons* for his town mansion.

The curator of Crozat's art collection was Charles de la Fosse and it was he who sponsored Watteau's second approach to the Academy in 1712. On this occasion, the committee was sufficiently impressed to offer him full membership and they took the unprecedented step of allowing him to paint a subject of his own choosing for his reception piece. Watteau needed

fathers of the Rococo style of decoration. Accordingly, Watteau joined the select team of painters who executed Audran's Arabesque designs in the royal and aristocratic residences which he had been commissioned to adorn. In his work for Audran between 1707-08, Watteau rapidly displayed his taste for innovation. At the château of La Muette, for example, he introduced tiny Chinese motifs into his designs – one of the earliest examples of a feature that was to prove so popular later in the century.

Audran also exerted an indirect but more profound influence on his pupil's development. In his role as curator of the Luxembourg Palace, he gave Watteau access to Rubens' majestic *Marie de Medici* cycle. This proved an inspiration to him. He made exhaustive sketches from the paintings and absorbed into his own style something of the master's brilliant handling and rich colouration.

GAINING INDEPENDENCE

Like many of his artistic associations, Watteau's stay with Audran was characteristically brief, lasting no more than a year, but it may have encouraged him to establish his independence more formally. In 1709, he entered for the Prix de Rome at the Academy, but failed to win this coveted award, with its promise of a trip to Italy. In all probability, the Biblical theme stipulated by the judging panel did not suit Watteau's talents.

In the same year, the artist returned home to Valenciennes. Perhaps he was disillusioned by his failure at the Academy or perhaps he was simply on the scent of a new departure in his career. French defeats at Oudenarde (1708) and Malplaquet (1709) had given military scenes a new topicality. A Paris dealer named Sirois purchased two such works from Watteau and there was a

Claude Gillot

Born in eastern France, Claude Gillot (1673-1722) came to Paris to study under Thomas Corneille, the prolific and skilled theatrical artisan. Gillot built up a successful career as a decorative painter and his Arabesques enjoyed a high reputation. Like Watteau, Gillot took five years to complete his reception piece for the Academy, although in his case, this was probably due to the thoroughly unsuitable subject – *Christ about to be Nailed to the Cross.* His theatrical scenes predated those of his pupil Watteau but lacked their compositional flair. After the departure of Watteau, Gillot painted less, concentrating more on his fine, spirited etchings. Gillot's inventory shows, rather poignantly, that several Italian Comedy pictures were left unfinished at his death.

five years, rather than the statutory two, to complete this formality, but the wait was worthwhile. When his *Pilgrimage to the Island of Cythera* (pp.26-7) was presented, in 1717, it earned a new classification in the Academy, that of the *fête galante*.

In the intervening period, Watteau had been extremely busy. On the death of La Fosse in 1716, he moved into Crozat's house and took the opportunity to study his host's superb collection. With its fine examples of work by Titian, Veronese and Bassano, it proved an ample substitute for the lost trip to Italy.

THE FINAL YEARS

Watteau was constantly moving around and his chronic restlessness increased in his final years. He soon left Crozat to return to Sirois and, in 1718, moved yet again to stay with a friend called Vleughels. Then, in 1719, he travelled to England, almost certainly to consult the renowned physician, Dr Mead, about his worsening health. However, the harsh English winter only

Detail: Les Fêtes Vénitiennes/National Galleries of Scotland, Edinburgh

The artist as actor
(left) In this detail from his painting Les Fêtes Vénitiennes, *Watteau has included himself. He often included bagpipe players in his works, usually using an actor as the model. This work was painted c.1718, about three years before Watteau's death, so his somewhat haggard and melancholy expression may indicate the effects of the illness that was to kill him.*

exacerbated his condition and, by 1720, he was back in Paris, staying with Edme Gersaint, Sirois' son-in-law. Gersaint was also an art dealer and, for his shop, Watteau painted the huge sign that was his final masterpiece (pp.34-5). Soon after, he moved to a house in the country, at Nogent, and asked Gersaint to sell off his effects, so that he could make one final journey to Valenciennes.

He must have realized that it was not to be. At Nogent, he destroyed a number of erotic paintings – it is thought, due to the visit of a priest – and began work on a 'Christ on the Cross'. Gersaint visited him there every few days and it was in his arms that Watteau died on 18 July 1721, at the age of 37, tragically young for one so gifted.

Death in Nogent
(below) Seeking relief from Paris, Watteau moved to a house in Nogent sur Marne. Intending to return to Valenciennes, he ordered that all his effects be sold when it became clear that death was close. Too sick to travel, Watteau died in Nogent in the arms of his friend Gersaint on 18 July 1721.

The Quarrel of the Cabmen
(left) This scene is taken from a pantomime by Regnard, which was first performed in 1695. Gillot has here produced a textual illustration – one that is meaningless outside the framework of the play. In contrast, Watteau's paintings were self-contained.

Lover of the theatre
(above) Claude Gillot was not only a painter and etcher but also a fine draughtsman. His love of the Commedia dell'Arte *is reflected in his surviving works. By exposing his pupil, Watteau, to the theatre he helped inspire some of the greatest paintings of the subject.*

Actors in a Landscape

The multi-faceted, luminous paintings for which Watteau is renowned were highly influential both in their own right and as the creation of a progressive artist who insisted on artistic autonomy.

Bildarchiv Preussischer Kulturbesitz

Gemäldegalerie, Staatliche Museum, Berlin

getting this, since Watteau works according to his fancy and commissions do not really suit him.'

A similar attitude is evident from Watteau's relations with the Academy. When applying for membership, he persuaded them to waive their normal entry rules and allow him to choose his own subject matter for his reception piece, thereby striking an important blow for artistic liberty.

Watteau's very personal style evolved from a wide variety of influences. To his Flemish origins he owed his taste for the naturalism of David Teniers and Adriaen van Ostade. This manifested itself most obviously in his early military pictures, but was still clearly present at the end of his life in the *Enseigne de Gersaint* (pp.34-5) which was essentially a monumental genre scene.

From his teacher Claude Gillot, Watteau

A magical touch
(left) Watteau's gift for rendering the delicacy of skin, hair and fine material is exemplified by the porcelain figure of 'Iris', who dances to the music of her friends.

The Country Dance
(below) The initial influence of Dutch genre painting on Watteau's art is clear in this rustic peasant scene, which he painted in his early years in Paris.

During his lifetime, Watteau's devotees instinctively recognized the importance of his art. They therefore tolerated his personal vagaries, and gave him unstinting practical and moral support as he pursued his particular artistic interests very much on his own terms.

Yet, loyal as Watteau's admirers had been in his lifetime, his reputation waned appreciably after his death. His two main followers, Jean Baptiste Pater and Nicolas Lancret – who had been his pupils – captured the outward form but not the spiritual core of his work and, as a result, later critics passed over all the *fêtes galantes* as shallow and frivolous exercises in decoration. During the Revolutionary period, Academy students even used his *Pilgrimage to the Island of Cythera* for target practice, hurling bread pellets at it.

When Watteau's popularity revived, it was on the strength of his modernity. He was one of the first artists to maintain a truly independent status, reluctant to submit either to the wishes of his patrons or to those of the Royal Academy in Paris. A letter from the French art dealer Sirois to a fellow dealer confirms this. In it, Sirois mentions how a client had asked Watteau to paint a specific scene from a play. 'But', Sirois writes, 'he has no hope of

Gift of Mrs. Herman C. Krannert

Indianapolis Museum of Art

Cailleux Collection, Paris

The Cajoler
(left) Watteau painted a series of eight decorative panels in about 1708, for a room in the Hôtel de Nointel in Paris. The carefully posed figures and graceful border are strongly reminiscent of his master, Claude Gillot.

La Toilette
(right) Painted 4 years before Watteau died, this delightful study reveals a new realism which was to inspire other 18th century artists to explore the same theme.

The Music Party
(below) This overtly theatrical composition places the figures on a 'stage' delineated by the marble columns and floor of the Tuileries colonnade, an imaginary landscape as backdrop. The audience includes the figure of Watteau's friend Vleughels on the far left.

Wallace Collection

borrowed the theatrical ideas that were to provide the raw material for his *fêtes galantes*, although, in place of Gillot's rather formal approach, he substituted the relaxed and sensuous handling which he had learnt from his study of the Old Masters. Rubens, with his robustness and vigour – which must at first have seemed so strange to Watteau – was a particular favourite and, later, his palette gained a new, luminous quality when he came into contact with the Venetian paintings and the Van Dycks in the collection of his friend Pierre Crozat, a millionaire art connoisseur.

WATTEAU'S METHOD

The gorgeous colouring Watteau adopted, paid handsome dividends when he began to paint the brilliantly costumed figures of his *fêtes galantes*. These paintings can most simply be described as leisurely outdoor scenes, in which exotically dressed young people idle away the time, listening to music and indulging in subtly choreographed love-games.

There were precedents for this painting genre which Watteau must have been familiar with, but he characteristically included in it his own

Wallace Collection

distinctive features. He added characters and props from the Italian Comedy which increased the sense of artifice, but he underplayed this by dispensing with the most obvious theatrical elements: the stage scenery and the references to specific plays. He also mingled figures in modern ball dress and masquerade with the actors and, to this end, he kept a collection of costumes in his studio, using his friends as models. Some, like his friend Vleughels and Sirois' daughter, can be readily identified in his paintings.

Essentially, Watteau extracted from the theatre its air of performance. His sitters seem to be enacting their own miniature dramas, as they engage in amorous intrigues: a man serenading his lady; a woman rejecting an importunate admirer; a solitary figure glancing sadly across at the object of an unrequited love. To this end, Watteau exploited the nature of the Italian Comedy itself, for which there was no set script. The action depended on a group of stock characters (the jealous old husband, the quick-witted servant, the sighing lovers, and so forth) playing out a series of improvised scenes. Watteau captured such scenes to perfection. Even in a naturalistic work like the *Enseigne de Gersaint*, where all the figures are in modern dress, the underlying structure is theatrical. Each character seems linked to another by a chain of implied relationships or mutual interests.

A MELANCHOLY ATMOSPHERE

By these means, Watteau sought to convey a mood rather than a well-defined story and, invariably, this mood was a melancholy one. Many of his figures appear isolated, scarcely aware of their fellow actors in the composition, and, all too frequently, they have their backs turned towards us. The *Mezzetin* (p.32) is a typical example. Here, the musician plays to an unseen lady while, behind him, the statue of a woman faces stonily away into the distance, in an attitude of cold rejection.

Usually, the wistful atmosphere of the *fêtes galantes* is interpreted as a reflection of Watteau's sickly constitution. Love, happiness and health are portrayed with great poetic sensibility, but they are seen from a distance, as bounties which cannot be shared by the artist who depicts them. Even the players involved in the idylls seem aware that their happiness cannot last.

In part, this effect was achieved by Watteau's curious method of composition. He did not usually produce preparatory sketches for his pictures, but instead, assembled them from individual drawings, which he had collected over the years into large, bound volumes. As these drawings were exclusively of single figures or small groups, it is hardly surprising that the different elements in his paintings often failed to relate to each other fully. This was a consequence of which Watteau must have been aware, and, doubtless, sought to exploit.

His methods did cause him technical problems,

Watteau's Drawings

The poetic effects which Watteau achieved in his paintings, and on which his reputation rests, were only made possible by their firm basis in reality. From his earliest days, Watteau sketched tirelessly, both from life and from the Old Masters. The dealer Gersaint reported that Watteau actually preferred drawing to painting, since the brush slowed his hand, thus delaying the image he had in his mind. Following the lead of Rubens, Watteau chose to work predominantly with three colours of chalk – black for the hair and costumes, sanguine for the flesh tints and white for the highlights.

Seated Persian
(left) Watteau drew several members of a Persian delegation to Paris in 1715. Here he contrasts the ambassador's exotic garb with his mild, almost contemplative facial expression.

Two studies of women
(below) Sketches such as these, which Watteau made throughout his life, were the basis on which he constructed his paintings.

Tone and line
(far left) The clarity and care with which these heads are drawn suggest a date of about 1714. Watteau achieved glowing flesh tones by fusing red and white chalks, often with the aid of a moistened fingertip. The delicacy of the facial modelling is combined with bold, dark shading for the hair, and a sharp, fine line for the hat.

Mezzetin with guitar
(left) One of Watteau's favourite characters from the Commedia dell' Arte *is here given a speedy but assured treatment, notably in the beautifully rendered hands.*

Kneeling man
(above) Watteau made use of this sketch when painting Jupiter and Antiope. It is a superb example of the way he combined bold outline and delicate shading to give a stunning image packed with intense physical energy.

Old Savoyard
(right) Watteau made four drawings of this poor immigrant worker, each one depicting him with the same battered hat, ragged clothing and peepshow. Watteau endows him with a sweet, resigned dignity but does not sentimentalize his poverty.

Uffizi, Florence

however, most notably in marrying his sitters to their landscape backgrounds. For example, X-rays of *The Music Party* (p.17) have shown that Watteau changed his mind several times about how best to link the architecture with the woodland scene beyond. Originally, there was a group of figures on the right, at the edge of the portico, but he finally painted them out rather clumsily and inadequately.

IMPATIENCE WITH IMPERFECTION

Several of Watteau's friends expressed dismay that he was never satisfied with his work and was constantly tempted to change it. The young dealer, Gersaint, cited one occasion when Watteau actually destroyed a painting that was almost finished, despite being offered a most generous price for it. Gersaint obviously learnt from this experience, for, when another picture was about to suffer a similar fate, he snatched it from Watteau's hands and refused to let him have it again.

Gersaint's explanation for such rashness accords well with our knowledge of Watteau's temperament. 'His pictures reflect some of the impatience and inconstancy of his nature. An object in his field of vision for any length of time irritated him; he had a need to switch from subject to subject; he often began a composition already half-bored with its perfection'.

This impatience accounts for the slapdash approach which marred a number of Watteau's

Fête in a Park
(right and detail below) In this later fête galante, *the lighting is softly focused to spotlight each separate group – the children playing with a dog, the people seated in the near and far ground, the statue – so that the eye is caught by and travels from one point of interest to the next. The beautiful perspective through the trees provides a welcome sense of space and freshness. Watteau's tiny figures, as always when examined closely, have a sharpness, realism and vivacity all their own.*

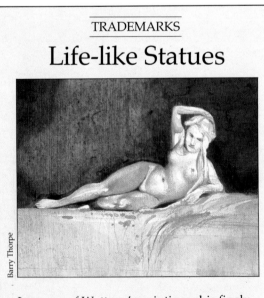

Barry Thorpe

TRADEMARKS

Life-like Statues

In many of Watteau's paintings, his finely-dressed, dainty and apparently decorous young people are overlooked by extraordinarily life-like statues of women. In a strange visual irony, these figures of stone are endowed with all the fleshly reality of a nude painted from life. They are more 'human' to us than the participants of the *fêtes galantes*, who are caught by the demands of time and social conventions.

Wallace Collection

Open-air Idylls

Watteau's *fêtes galantes* have a long pedigree. In Venice in the early 16th century, Giorgione and Palma Vecchio produced evocative Arcadian scenes where figures in modern dress linger in a carefree fashion. Rubens expanded on the theme, adding an amorous slant in his playful depictions of the Garden of Love.

Josef S. Martin/Artothek

Prado, Madrid

works. He had a tendency to overload his brush with oil, since this allowed him to spread his colours more rapidly. Unfortunately, his brush sometimes became clogged which would result in unsightly trails of paint smudging his canvases.

Even more disastrous was his habit of 'oiling out' (overpainting with a fresh coat of oil) those sections of a picture which displeased him, and then covering them with a new layer of paint, before the old surface had dried. Thus, when the oil did eventually dry, the old colours began to show through from underneath. From as early as the 1740s, this sort of deterioration was noted in many of his works and Louis XV was actively advised against buying pictures by Watteau for this reason.

Fortunately, these defects did not blind later critics to the unique qualities of Watteau's genius, or prevent him from winning the admiration of artists as diverse as Boucher, Monet and Turner.

England in fact responded with immediate and sustained enthusiasm to Watteau's art. Gainsborough frankly made use of his compositional technique, and the habitually circumspect Reynolds gave him an exceptionally warm accolade when he said, 'Watteau is a master whom I adore'.

In Germany, meanwhile, Frederick the Great avidly collected Watteau's pictures, to amass what still remains today the finest and most representative range of the artist's work.

Peter Paul Rubens (1577-1640) **Garden of Love**
(above) The ebullience of Rubens' work, with its lolling, amorous men and women, tumbling cupids and erotic symbolism, differs dramatically from Watteau's own style.

Giorgione (c.1476-1510) **Fête Champêtre**
(below) Watteau probably knew this beautiful painting. He took up the idea it expressed, of the liberating power of nature, but injected it with the vitality he got from Rubens.

Lauros-Giraudon

Louvre, Paris

THE MAKING OF A MASTERPIECE

The Pilgrimage to the Island of Cythera

The presentation of this painting to the Royal Academy in Paris in August 1717, set the seal on Watteau's membership of that distinguished body. The work had taken five years to deliver, but once the committee grew impatient, Watteau completed it rapidly in eight months. Officials shortened the title to 'fête galante' thereby creating some of the later confusion as to the precise subject of the picture.

Watteau probably took his theme from the final scene of Florence Dancourt's play 'Les Trois Cousines', in which a group of friends make a pilgrimage to the Island of Cythera – Venus's island – to find their partners. As usual, Watteau's real subject is a mood rather than an action. The mellow autumn colour and the glowing sunset convey a feeling of the transience of human happiness. Only the couple on the far right, still spellbound by love, seem unaware of this.

Ulysse Moussalli Collection

Bulloz

Lauros-Giraudon

Oil study

(above right) Watteau rarely made specific studies for his paintings. That he did so in this case, shows how important was the end result.

On the brink of departure

(right) Boatmen and cupids dominate the couples as they leave the island, a compositional signal that we are witnessing the end of their story.

Bon Voyage

(below) Claude Audran made this engraving after the Cythera. *It is directly inspired by the lingering couple on the far right of the original.*

Jean-Loup Charmet

Staatliche Schlosser und Garten, Schloss Charlottenburg, Berlin

Preliminary sketch
(below left) Because of
the complexity of the
composition, Watteau
made several preparatory
sketches of the figures he
wished to include.

The Berlin version
(above) Watteau made
this copy of the Louvre
painting for his friend,
Julienne. But it lacks
the restraint and wistful
beauty of his original.

A rueful glance
(below) The sad,
backward glance of the
woman at the centre of
the composition adds
poignancy to the moment
when the lovers leave.

Louvre, Paris

British Museum

'The great poet of the 18th
century is Watteau.'

Edmond and Jules de Goncourt

Gallery

Watteau is considered one of the greatest painters of the Rococo era, a time when delicacy and refinement held sway. Whereas most Rococo art is associated with frivolity, however, Watteau often conveyed a profound sense of melancholy – his figures may be engaged in sensuous pursuits, but we sense that all such pleasures are transient.

La Partie Quarrée (The Foursome) *c.1713*
19¾" × 25½" Fine Arts Museum, San Francisco

This painting has many of the features that were to become characteristic of Watteau – fashionable young people in masquerade costume in a garden setting, exquisitely painted materials, a guitar, and a suggestion of amorous involvement without anything explicit. The back view of the standing figure gives him an enigmatic quality.

The Pilgrimage to the Island of Cythera is the most haunting example of his ability to create a poignant dreamworld.

The artificial world of the theatre provided much of Watteau's subject matter, whether in groups such as Actors of the Comédie Française and Actors of the Comédie Italienne or single figures such as Mezzetin and Gilles. Music-making also was a favourite theme, as in La Gamme d'Amour.

The great work of the end of Watteau's career – L'Enseigne de Gersaint – seemed to herald a change of direction in his art, but his tragically early death prevented him from developing this new and more realistic style.

La Gamme d'Amour (The Scale of Love) *c.1715*
20″ × 23½″ National Gallery, London

The title, like that of most of Watteau's pictures, comes from an engraving published after his death. It refers to the musical scales, music being, in Shakespeare's words, 'the food of love'. The two main figures occur in other works by Watteau; the significance of the various figures in the background is uncertain.

25

Antoine Watteau

**The Pilgrimage to the Island
of Cythera** *c.1718*
50¾″ × 76¾″ Charlottenburg Castle,
West Berlin

*This is a variant of the painting (now in the
Louvre) that Watteau presented to the
Academy as his reception piece in 1717.
Cythera is the island where, according to
legend, Venus came ashore after being born
from the waves, and so was a place of
pilgrimage for would-be lovers. A statue of
Venus is on the right. The original title of
the painting was L'Embarquement pour
l'Île de Cythère (The Embarkation for the
Island of Cythera), but it is now generally
agreed that the figures are returning from
the island rather than departing for it; the
men and women have clearly paired off and
are lingering rather than keen to depart.*

27

Young Couples with Guitarist and Shepherd c.1718
22″ × 31¾″ Charlottenburg Castle, West Berlin

The theme of lovers in a parkland setting has had a long vogue in European painting (it goes back to a medieval type known as The Garden of Love), but Watteau was the artist who truly made it his own. Here he seems to be recalling the famous Fête Champêtre (Pastoral Concert) by Giorgione in the Louvre (p.21).

Dancing Couple, Bagpiper and Eight other Figures c.1717
22″ × 31¾″ Charlottenburg Castle, West Berlin

Watteau often repeated motifs or even entire compositions in his paintings and this is similar to a picture he did a year or two earlier, now in the Musée Condé at Chantilly. For all its artificiality, the painting has some beautifully observed expressions and details, such as the dog scratching itself in the foreground.

Actors of the Comédie Française *c.1716*
14½″ × 18¾″ Staatliche Museen, West Berlin

*This forms a contrast to the painting opposite. The Comédie Française,
the national theatre of France, was founded in 1680 by Louis XIV.
Watteau contrasts the formality of the French players (who seem to be
enacting a mythological scene involving Bacchus and Apollo) with the
more spontaneous charm of the Comédie Italienne, opposite.*

Actors of the Comédie Italienne *c.1718*
14½″ × 18¾″ Staatliche Museen, West Berlin

*The Comédie Italienne (or Commedia dell' Arte) represented a separate
theatrical tradition from the Comédie Française. Originating in Italy
and spreading throughout western Europe, it featured stereotyped
characters such as Harlequin. It often presented night performances
and Watteau has subtly portrayed the illumination of the torch.*

Mezzetin *c.1719*
21″ × 16¾″ Metropolitan Museum, New York

*Mezzetin or Mezzetino was one of the stock characters of the Italian
Comedy, which was a constant source of inspiration to Watteau. Here
he is seen as an ardent but hopeless lover serenading the unseen object
of his adoration. The picture is sometimes thought to be a portrait of the
actor Angelo Constantini, celebrated for his portrayal of Mezzetin.*

Gilles *c.1719*
72½″ × 58½″ Louvre, Paris

Pierrot (or Gilles, as he was usually called in France) was, like Mezzetin, one of the characters of the Italian Comedy. This painting was probably intended for use as a theatrical signboard. The figure has a boldness rare in Watteau's work and the broad handling of the paint suggests it was meant to be seen from a distance.

L'Enseigne de Gersaint (Gersaint's Signboard) *1721*
71¾″ × 121¼″ Charlottenburg Castle, West Berlin

Watteau painted this picture as a signboard for his friend Edme Gersaint, a picture dealer.
Gersaint himself said that Watteau painted it in eight days. The identity of the figures is
uncertain, but it is generally thought that Gersaint is the man holding the large oval picture,
and the young man in the centre is probably Watteau.

34

The 'Commedia dell'Arte'

**The improvised theatre of the *Commedia dell'Arte* entertained
generations of Italians and influenced dramatists and artists
throughout Europe. Its principal characters are still familiar today.**

Giancarlo Costa

Early theatre
*(right) Although its exact
origins remain obscure,
the* Commedia dell'Arte
*began as a form of street
theatre, with the actors
relying on their diverse
improvisational skills to
entertain the public.*

A pictorial record
*(left) The most popular
plays in the repertoire of
the* Commedia dell'Arte
*are recorded in a collection
of 17th-century
watercolours. This
illustration shows the
stage set for* The
Prisoners, *and gives an
insight into the farcical
nature of the plot.*

The works of Watteau are invariably peopled with
figures who act and are dressed as if in a play.
Many of these figures, both in their costume and
bearing, are in fact directly lifted from a form of
drama which, though in decline by Watteau's day,
had enjoyed a wide popularity since at least the
early 16th century.

This dramatic tradition, known generally as the
Commedia dell'Arte, is also referred to as *Commedia
all'Improviso*, *Commedia alle Maschere*, and *Commedia
Italiana*, terms which describe its principal features:
it was improvised, made use of masks, and was
developed and practised exclusively by Italians. Its
exact origins are disputed, and attempts have been
made to establish a link with the mime companies
of ancient Rome and the medieval mystery plays.
The only certainty is that the *Commedia dell'Arte*
was initially a form of street entertainment which
would probably have risen little above the level of
pantomime and buffoonery had it not been taken

up in the Renaissance by the Italian aristocracy, for
whom it provided a lively alternative to the written
drama known as the *Commedia Erudita*.

Whereas the *Commedia Erudita* was allowed to
be performed only by amateurs, the players of the
Commedia dell'Arte were all 'of the profession'
(*dell'Arte*) and needed not only highly developed
improvisational skills but also such diverse talents
as singing, miming, playing an instrument, and
performing acrobatics or tricks. A typical company
consisted of at least ten people, each of whom
specialized in one of several stock characters who
made up the *Commedia dell'Arte*. These characters
had costumes, masks and mannerisms that made
them immediately recognizable. Their names
might often be different and their appearance and
personality change, either under the influence of a
particular actor or in deference to regional tastes or
new fashions, but they remained fundamentally
the same from one play to the next.

Thus there were always the two *magnifici*, or elderly men, and two *zanni*, or servants. The pair of elderly men generally consisted of a Venetian merchant called Pantalon and a Bolognese doctor named Doctor Graziano. Pantalon represented the voice of authority, but was also made out to be a bit of a fool. Doctor Graziano meanwhile, was a loquacious pedant who spoke in riddles or tongue-twisters. The *zanni* acted as a Laurel and Hardy team, and always provided the play's main comic relief. Beyond this, however, it is difficult to generalize about them, as they took on many different names and identities, most notably Arlecchino (Harlequin), Pulcinella (Punch) and Pedrolino (later known as Pierrot or Gilles).

Another of the characters in the company was the Captain, who often went by the name of

Jean-Loup Charmet

The comic plot
(above) Love and intrigue were the central themes in most of the plays. This 16th-century painting probably shows the celebrated Gelosi troupe, with the young heroine confronting her angry guardian, the frequently cuckolded Pantalone.

Il Capitano
(below) Known by many names, the Captain was a dreamer who lived in an imaginary world of his own heroics. Initially a complex character – often an unsuccessful lover who was cheated and ridiculed both by the ladies and the servants – he gradually degenerated into a clown, and by the mid-17th century had disappeared from the Italian theatre, only to be replaced by the more sophisticated Scaramouche.

Giancarlo Costa

Mauro Pucciarelli

Arlecchino
(left) The most famous character of the Commedia dell'Arte, *Arlecchino – or Harlequin – is* instantly recognizable by his patchwork costume. One of the two *zanni, he relied on his wit and acrobatic abilities to provide much of the comic relief.*

Museo Burcardo, Rome

Captain Spavento del Vall'Inferno. He was portrayed as a braggart and coward, and was clearly intended as a satire on one of the hated Spanish soldiers of 16th-century Italy. A later and more subtle variant of this character was Scaramouche, who was depicted partly as a sad and foolish Captain and partly as a wise and merry *zanni*. Finally there was a servant-woman, who functioned as a confidante, and two pairs of lovers, who were acted unmasked by the most handsome members of the company.

Although improvised, the *Commedia dell'Arte* plays closely followed written plots that became almost as standardized as the characters who enacted them. The plays, whether comical, tragical, historical, pastoral, or a combination of all four, dwelt principally on love, in particular on the difficulties barring the happiness of young lovers. The actors, when not rehearsing, spent much of their time reading elevating literature such as

Giancarlo Costa

later, in the 1650s, they were offered a permanent base in the French capital, a base which they shared at first with Molière and the company of his which later emerged as their great rival, the *Comédie Française*.

DRAMATIC EVOLUTION

Even in France the Italian troupes continued to perform their plays in Italian, a language which if known at all to the French public, was rarely understood by them in all its regional and colloquial nuances. Snatches of French dialogue eventually had to be introduced into the plays, together with other, less obvious concessions to French taste. These changes allowed the Italians to maintain their popularity with the French, but at the same time fundamentally altered the character of the *Commedia dell'Arte*. For instance, whereas the plays had once been very much of a group effort, they now came to be dominated by virtuoso single performances given by celebrated actors such as Tiberio Fiorillo (the man who popularized Scaramouche) and Domenico Biancolelli (famous for his Harlequins), both of whom abandoned their masks so as to develop a more expressive style of playing.

In addition, the plays came to be increasingly dependent on song and dance and rejected the simple props of earlier days in favour of elaborate stage machinery. Yet another innovation – topical social satire often directed at specific members of the audience – had the more immediate effect of having the Italian players expelled from France in 1697 following the production of *La Fausse Prude* in the presence of Louis XIV's wife (and former mistress), Madame de Maintenon.

When Watteau first came to Paris in 1702 the Italian players were still in exile. Like many of his

A joint venture
(above) In the mid-17th century the Commedia dell'Arte *was given a permanent base in Paris. This 17th-century painting commemorates over 60 years of comedy in France and shows the French actors of Molière's company and their Italian counterparts playing the traditional roles.*

The ancestor of Punch
(above) Pulcinella was portrayed as a cowardly fool and a vicious rogue. Originally Harlequin's chief rival, he became a major figure in French and English comedy.

treatises on love in order to improve the quality of their improvised dialogue. However, too much talk tended to bore the restless audiences, whom the actors then had to placate by resorting to ever more ingenious and desperate measures: blatantly erotic scenes, occasionally even involving nudity, always proved popular with the public, but naturally provoked the clergy's wrath.

The dangers in attending a *Commedia dell'Arte* performance, however, were perhaps not so much moral as physical. Actors, and especially actresses, feeling that their colleagues were hogging too much of the lime-light, would sometimes start fighting on stage, inspiring the audience soon to follow suit. By the beginning of the 17th century, the performances had acquired such an emotive character that severe, punitive measures had to be introduced: heckling or jeering was punishable by fines, torture, and imprisonment; fist-fighting or throwing apples, nuts, chestnuts and other such objects at the actors resulted in five years in the galleys; and taking out one's sword led to summary execution.

TOURING COMPANIES

The *Commedia dell'Arte* companies were always travelling, not only throughout Italy, but also the rest of Europe, influencing dramatists of the calibre of Shakespeare, Lope de Vega and Molière. In France, which they first visited in the 1570s on the invitation of Henry III, they found perhaps their most enthusiastic audiences. Almost a century

Antoine Watteau

generation, he probably had very sentimental notions about what their style of acting was like, and longed for their return. This did not happen until 1716, by which date their improvised plays had begun to seem old-fashioned. Anxious not to be banished again, they looked for new material, and chose to put on a French play written by an obscure painter called Jacques Autreau. This play, which overcame the problems caused by the Italians' inadequate command of French by dealing with a group of foreigners stranded in a French port, immediately revived box-office takings and the company's popularity.

This success was followed shortly afterwards by that of a play written by a French dramatist frequently compared with Watteau, Marivaux. The very title of this work, *Harlequin refined by Love*, is an indication of the great changes which the *Commedia dell'Arte* characters had undergone by this date. The once crude and always boisterous *zanni* had now become refined beings capable even of great sadness. In Watteau's famous *Gilles* (p.33) a stock figure from the *Commedia dell'Arte* has been transformed into an image which was to have a far greater appeal to later tastes – that of the tragic clown.

A theatrical family
(above) The Biancolelli family provided the theatre with great actors for over a century. Domenico, shown here in the role of Doctor Graziano, was renowned for his characterization of Harlequin, and died from a chill after an energetic performance in front of the King.

Expulsion from France
(left) As performances grew more sophisticated, topical satire became an important element of the comedy. One such attack against Louis XIV's wife Madame de Maintenon resulted in the closing of the Commedia dell'Arte *at the Hôtel de Bourgogne and the expulsion of the players from Paris in 1697.*

The tragic clown
(right) Watteau's painting The Italian Comedians *shows the refined figure of Pierrot surrounded by the company of Luigi Riccoboni, who brought the players back to Paris in 1716. Derived from the* zanni *Pedrolino, the character of Pierrot was introduced by Molière in the mid-17th century.*

A Year in the Life 1720

During Watteau's visit to England in 1720, the atmosphere must have seemed uncannily like that of his native France. Both countries were gripped by a mania for financial speculation, followed in short order by a panic when the 'bubbles' burst.

In Britain, 1720 was long remembered as 'South Sea Year'. Although institutions such as the Bank of England and the Stock Exchange were only a few years old, the British had already acquired a taste for speculation. This reached a peak in 1720, when the South Sea company offered to take over a substantial part of the National Debt, an apparently splendid piece of financial planning. In reality it was a thoroughly unsound operation that could only be sustained while the price of South Sea stock kept rising.

Nevertheless, in February 1720 Parliament accepted the scheme with an enthusiasm partly inspired by a lavish distribution of 'complimentary' shares among chosen MPs who encouraged the public to buy; South Sea shares boomed. From a figure of 130 on the stock market early in the year they reached

Prado, Madrid

AISA

Family ambitions

(above) When Philip V's first wife died in 1714 leaving two sons, the Spanish King made the unfortunate mistake of marrying Isabella Farnese, a singularly ambitious female who was determined to secure the dukedoms of Parma and Tuscany for her two sons from the marriage. Spain invaded Sardinia and Sicily to that end but in 1720 was forced by the Quadruple Alliance of Austria, France, Britain and Holland to hand back her conquests in return for the succession to the Italian Dukedoms.

Michael Holford

Royal sculptor

(left) Antoine Coysevox, the French sculptor, died in 1720 at the age of 80. In 1666 he had been appointed sculptor to Louis XIV and by 1679 he was working hard at Versailles. This dramatic Baroque relief of his patron in the Salon de Guerre is one of his masterworks. Others include the tomb of Cardinal Mazarin and a number of superbly sculpted busts. With these later portrait heads, he changed his style, dropping the formality of the Baroque in favour of a lighter approach, anticipatory of the Rococo.

Speculative disaster

(above) By December 1720 France was in financial chaos. Five years before, John Law, an emigré Scot, had begun his masterplan to regenerate the French economy and eliminate the national debt. A bank was set up with 75 per cent of its capital in government bills. This was then linked to Law's newly founded Mississippi Company which gradually gained a monopoly of foreign trade. Speculation grew apace and vast fortunes were made – while many thousands were ruined.

400 in May. Whenever their impetus seemed to be fading, a new share issue stimulated another wave of buying and a consequent rise in share values. The hitherto exclusively male preserve of Exchange Alley, where the London stockbrokers had their offices, was invaded by women of fashion in search of thrills and ladies of easy virtue bent on investing their protectors' benefactions.

STOCK MARKET CATASTROPHE

On 17 August, South Sea shares reached the fantastic figure of 900; and then the bubble burst. Within six weeks the price was down to 190, and before the end of the year it had fallen to 135. Suicides and bankruptcies multiplied, and Parliament – full of out-of-pocket Commons Members and peers – as a result, confiscated the bulk of the directors' estates.

The infuriated Members were also determined to find political scapegoats and as it soon became clear that the directors had disbursed well over a million pounds in bribes and 'loans', a prodigious scandal seemed imminent. Both the court and the cabinet were deeply involved, but they found an able defender in Robert Walpole, who had become Paymaster General in June 1720. He successfully defended the chief minister, Sunderland, and restored public confidence in the economy. However, Walpole was unable to save all his colleagues, despite the fact that the company's cashier had fled abroad, taking with him the most incriminating ledgers.

Oddly enough, nobody in Britain seems to have taken

An extraordinary monarch
(left) *A man of demonic energy, Peter the Great was supremely conscious of Russia's destiny. He laboured hard to build up the armed forces, even working as a shipwright and serving in the lower ranks himself. By 1720 the Great Northern War against Sweden was almost at an end, with Russia as victor.*

Countess Bobrinskoy Collection

The 'South Sea Bubble'
(above) *This collage of contemporary satire celebrates the disastrous fever of speculation which gripped England in 1720. The collapse of the South Sea Company led to the ruination of many and the fortune of a few.*

warning from the fate of John Law's ventures in Paris. Law was a Scot who had fled abroad after killing a rival in love during an impromptu duel in Bloomsbury Square. Having made a fortune as a gambler, he formed the Mississippi Company linking it with his newly founded bank which soon achieved national status. Paper money issued by the bank became the official currency, and at the beginning of 1720 Law was appointed *Contrôleur général* of all French government finances. Many of his ideas were sound, but over-ambition created a massive wave of speculation. So much money was printed that France suffered the first serious inflation of modern times. In May, when Law reacted by announcing a devaluation, public confidence in him evaporated. He was dismissed, and his company, bank and currency collapsed. In December he fled from France, never to return.

A treaty signed in 1720 ended one of the more curious European wars, fought by Spain against the Quadruple Alliance of Britain, France, Austria and Holland. In effect, these great powers combined to stop Spain upsetting the general peace settlement of 1713. Nevertheless, the Spanish Queen, Isabella Farnese, achieved one of her aims: her son Charles was granted the succession to the Italian states of Parma, Piacenza and Tuscany. Since Philip V of Spain had sons by his first wife, the strong-minded Isabella had determined to find thrones for his own children, and her career proved a triumph of sheer persistence. It took thirty years of war, starting with the Spanish invasion of Sicily and Sardinia, but by 1748 both her sons were enthroned in Italian principalities.

Imperial Baroque

(right) Generally acknowledged as the masterpiece of the Austrian architect Johann Fischer von Erlach (1656-1723), the Karlskirche was under construction from 1715 to 1739, the original design being seen through to completion by his son. The church was commissioned in fulfilment of a vow made by the Holy Roman Emperor Charles VI in connection with a plague outbreak in Vienna in 1713 and dedicated to Saint Charles Borromeo. The charitable exploits of the saint are illustrated in spiral form on the two columns that flank the main porch, in imitation of the Emperor Trajan's column in Rome – impressive symbols of Hapsburg imperial authority.

ZEFA Picture Library

Lauros-Giraudon

Versailles

The Regency of Louis XV

(left) Louis XIV died in 1715, to be succeeded by his great-grandson Louis XV, a delicate child of five who would not attain his legal majority until 1723. Philip, Duke of Orleans, nephew to the late king, had been appointed to preside over the council of regency but, with the connivance of the Paris Parlement, he succeeded in becoming sole regent to the boy king in return for restoring their right of remonstrance. Parlement used their newly won right to attack government financial policy, which resulted in their exile to Pontoise in 1720. There they were bullied into accepting the papal bull Unigenitus *which condemned the Jansenists and saw the collapse of Law's* Système.

Chardin: self-portrait/Louvre, Paris

Chardin

1699-1779

Chardin stands out as the great individualist of French 18th-century painting. Although he was a contemporary of Boucher and Fragonard and worked at a time when the florid Rococo style and erotic and mythological subjects were the height of fashion, Chardin achieved his fame with quiet still-lifes and homely genre scenes painted with a directness and simplicity that made them appeal to the bourgeoisie and royalty alike.

Chardin spent his entire life in his native Paris. He never seems to have felt the need to travel abroad or to delve into the art of the past for his inspiration, preferring to find the material for his paintings in his own well-ordered household. But subject-matter was always secondary to Chardin's search for compositional perfection and harmony of colour and tone, and few artists have matched his purely painterly achievements.

43

The Quiet Parisian

Chardin's candid and unpretentious artistic vision reflected some of his own best qualities and those of the bourgeois world to which he belonged – qualities of honesty, thrift and domestic contentment.

Key Dates

1699 born in Paris

1724 enrols with the Guild of St Luke

1728 elected member of the Academy

1731 marries Marguerite Saintard; son, Jean-Pierre, born

1733 begins to paint genre scenes

1735 Marguerite dies

1743 made Councillor of the Academy

1744 marries Françoise Marguerite Pouget

1752 granted a pension by the King

1754 Jean-Pierre wins the Prix de Rome

1755 elected Treasurer of the Academy

1762 Jean-Pierre kidnapped by pirates

1779 dies in Paris

Lauros-Giraudon

The Swing; Louvre, Paris

A tutor's example

(above) Chardin's teacher, Cazes, could not afford models for his students. Instead they spent hours fruitlessly copying his own paintings, such as the one shown here.

Chardin's Paris

*(right) 'Genre painters',
wrote the Goncourt
brothers in the 19th
century, 'are for preference
and almost naturally born
in Paris.' Whether this is
true or not, Chardin had
this 'ideal' start in life.
Appropriately, he was
born on the Left Bank,
which was — and long
remained — the city's
artistic quarter. Although
destined to take up his
father's craft of carpentry,
Chardin's artistic bent
was evidently so strong
that by the age of 18 he
had begun his
apprenticeship with the
court painter, Pierre-
Jacques Cazes.*

Jean-Baptiste-Siméon Chardin was born in Paris in the artists' quarter of Saint-Germain-des-Prés on 2 November 1699. His father, Jean, was a carpenter who made billiard tables for the King, and he naturally assumed that his eldest son would follow his trade. Accordingly, the young Chardin was given the kind of practical education suitable for a craftsman. However, he must have shown an early talent for painting and rebelled against his father's plans as he was apprenticed at the age of 18 to the court painter Pierre-Jacques Cazes, who specialized in large religious works.

Cazes's teaching methods were extremely uninspiring. Because he was too poor to employ a model, Cazes set his students the dull task of copying engravings and Chardin was later to complain that this procedure would never prepare any painter for the important business of observing nature. Chardin seems to have had a further period of study with the artist Nicolas Coypel, who first awakened his interest in still life by asking him to paint a gun in one of his portraits, but Chardin was, for the most part, self-taught.

By the time he was in his mid-20s, Chardin had established himself as a still-life painter. In 1724, he enrolled as a Master Painter in the Guild of St Luke. This was really a craftsman's organization – a poor relation to the Academy, with none of its rival's intellectual prestige. By joining the Guild,

Explorer Archives

Musée Carnavalet, Paris

Lauros-Giraudon

The Skate
(below) This painting won
the admiration of the
famous artist, Nicolas de
Largillière, and other
academicians when they
saw it in the annual
exhibition at the Place
Dauphine. They
encouraged Chardin to
apply for membership to
the Academy, and, on 25
September 1728, he was
received as a painter of
animals and fruit.

The artist's wife
(above) Chardin married
Marguerite Saintard after
an engagement of several
years. Their modest home
included Chardin's studio
where he painted his
genre scenes. In this
painting the model is
quite possibly Marguerite,
and the simplicity and
tranquillity of the scene
reflect the contentment of
the couple's tragically
brief marriage.

**Restoration work at
Fontainebleau**
(below) On their marriage,
Chardin and his wife were
relatively poor, so he
gladly seized the
opportunity to earn extra
money by helping the
painter Jean-Baptiste van
Loo carry out restoration
work in the Francis I
Gallery at Fontainebleau.
This did, however, keep
him from his own painting
for a while.

possibly at the insistence of his father, Chardin
was indicating that he was a practical man, capable
of earning a living by his skill.

This was an important consideration, for by this
time the young artist was engaged to Marguerite
Saintard, whom he had met at a local dance.
Although the marriage contract was drawn up in
1723, the wedding was delayed as Chardin's
financial circumstances were too insecure to satisfy
the bride's wealthy father. In the meantime,
Chardin attempted to eke a living by painting
details and accessories in works by more famous
artists and by fulfilling the occasional commission.

A FIRST SUCCESS

One such commission gave Chardin his first
glimmer of public recognition. A surgeon friend of
his father's asked him to paint a signboard for his
shop, but instead of painting the usual still-life of
blades and scalpels, Chardin produced a busy
figure composition showing a wounded man
being brought to a surgeon. He hung it outside the
shop at the dead of night. The surgeon may have
been a little surprised at the view that greeted him
the next day, but his annoyance abated when he
saw the number of passers-by who paused outside
to admire the picture.

It was in the mid-1720s that Chardin started
exhibiting his paintings at the Exposition de la
Jeunesse, an open-air exhibition for young
unknown artists held annually at the Place
Dauphine. In 1728 he showed several works
including *The Skate* (below left), and the famous
painter Nicolas de Largillière, who happened to be
strolling by, was so impressed that he encouraged
the young artist to present his work at the
Academy.

Not quite believing this sudden and
unexpected honour, Chardin devised a way of

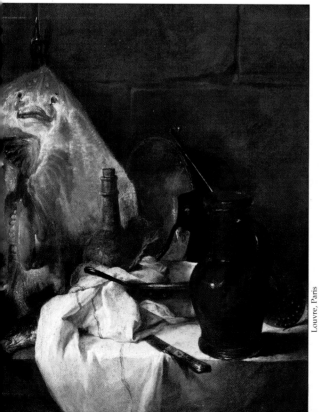

Contemporary Still-life Painters

When Chardin began his career as an artist, still-life and animal painting in France was dominated by Alexandre-François Desportes (1661-1743) and Jean-Baptiste Oudry (1686-1755). Both artists painted animals and hunting scenes for the King, as well as grand set-pieces showing fruit and dead game. As the older of the two, Desportes was really Oudry's predecessor, but while their careers overlapped, the two men were rivals. Chardin, it seems, thought highly of them both, although the modest scope of his mature work is very different from their elaborate and aristocratic canvases.

Wallace Collection, London

Desportes: Dogs, Dead Game and Fruit
(above) Desportes' style was based on 17th-century Flemish painting and had a strong naturalistic element. The affinity Chardin felt for it is underlined by the fact that he owned two copies of pictures after Desportes.

Oudry: The Dead Wolf
(below) Influenced by his teacher, the famous Largillière, Oudry tended to adopt a fanciful style with high key Rococo colouring. Chardin's early paintings show a definite awareness of Oudry's still-lifes, which combined grandeur with well-observed detail.

Wallace Collection, London

testing the true opinion of the Academy. He went there, hung his paintings in an obscure position in one of the small rooms and waited nearby. Largillière once again picked out Chardin's pictures for special praise, remarking to a friend that they must be by a Flemish master. When Chardin stepped forward and declared that the paintings were his, Largillière urged him to apply at once for membership of the Academy. That September, Chardin was accepted into the Academy as a painter of flowers, fruit and genre subjects. He offered *The Skate* (pp.44-5) and *The Buffet* as his reception pieces.

In 1731, Chardin and his fiancée were finally married in the neighbourhood church of Saint Sulpice. The long engagement was probably brought to its conclusion by a sudden slump in the fortunes of Marguerite's family, but this meant that the bride's dowry was less than expected, and Chardin had to find some way of making extra money. When he was offered the chance to help Jean-Baptiste van Loo restore the Francis I Gallery at Fontainebleau, Chardin accepted eagerly, even though it was a diversion from painting.

DOMESTIC HAPPINESS

The young couple made their modest home in the Chardin family house in the Rue Princesse, where they occupied three rooms, and where Chardin kept his studio on the top floor. The marriage was a brief one – Marguerite died tragically early in 1735 – but the domestic happiness it brought Chardin is evident in the genre scenes that he began to paint at about this time. It is tempting to see some of the women in them as Marguerite, and Chardin's two children, Jean-Pierre and Marguerite Agnès, must have served as models on many occasions.

The reasons for the change of direction in Chardin's art have never been fully explained,

The ultimate seal of approval
(right) Chardin's popularity grew steadily in the 1740s and '50s, and one of his most enthusiastic patrons was Louis XV, who crowned his purchases by granting the artist a pension of 500 francs in 1752. The seal was set on Chardin's success when he was given lodgings in the Louvre (shown here). In the previous century it had been the royal residence, and it still housed the magnificent art collection amassed by the monarchy, which would become public property in 1793.

A. Wolf/Explorer

Louvre, Paris

routine, her manners, her daily occupations, her morals, the moods of her children, her furniture, her wardrobe.'

But it was not just the Parisian bourgeoisie that enjoyed the paintings. Chardin's patrons eventually included several European aristocrats and even royalty. After his meeting with Chardin in 1740, Louis XV began to take a keen interest in the artist's work, and when the Swedish princess, Louise Ulrique, saw the two Chardins owned by her ambassador in Paris, she asked him to commission two similar scenes from the artist for her palace at Drottingholm.

The unfortunate princess had to wait over a year before her paintings were completed. Chardin's proverbial slowness annoyed his patrons and meant that his income was never as high as it might have been. But his material comforts were assured when, in his mid-40s, he married Françoise Marguerite Pouget, a wealthy widow of 37 with no children and a steady income from the property she owned.

Despite occasional accusations of laziness from critics because of his meagre output, Chardin continued to work steadily throughout the 1740s and 1750s. Royal favours and official approval grew. In 1743, the artist was made a Councillor of the Academy, and in 1755, he was unanimously elected its Treasurer. A few years later, Chardin was given the extra responsibility of deciding how the pictures should be hung at exhibition. He fulfilled the duties of these posts with fairness and

An invaluable friend

(above) It was thanks to a hint from his friend and fellow artist, Aved, that Chardin was spurred into attempting the 'higher' art of figure painting. He had a considerable gift for genre portraits, as is shown in this affectionate portrait of Aved himself.

Chardin's second wife

(below right) Chardin married for the second time in early middle age. His new wife was a widow of 37, Françoise Marguerite Pouget, who had her own property and income. Chardin drew this late portrait of her in 1776, when he had begun working in pastels.

although it is said to have been a remark by the portraitist Aved, who shared Chardin's studio, that spurred him into action. When Aved refused a commission to paint a lady's portrait for 400 livres because the price was too low, Chardin urged him to reconsider, saying that it was always worth making 400 livres. Aved replied haughtily, 'That would be true if a portrait were as easy to make as a sausage!', referring to the still-life that was on Chardin's easel.

The sarcastic aside had a fortunate result. Chardin began painting homely kitchen and genteel drawing room scenes which earned him enormous popularity. He soon began to have his exhibited pictures engraved, often accompanied by a verse, so that his compositions reached a wider audience than just the visitors to his exhibitions at the Salon. The subjects of these genre scenes were ones that could be widely appreciated. As a contemporary pamphlet stated: 'There is not a single housewife who does not see in them an impression of herself, her domestic

Louvre, Paris

Life-long Associates

Chardin's art was ensured a wide audience through the work of his engraver, Charles-Nicolas Cochin the Elder. His son Charles-Nicolas Cochin the Younger was a life-long friend of Chardin, and, as Secretary of the Academy from 1758, was ideally placed to foster the artist's interests. He obtained for Chardin the prestigious task of hanging pictures at the Academy, and he constantly agitated for an increase in Chardin's royal pension. He also negotiated the commissions which Chardin carried out at the châteaux of Choisy and Bellevue in the mid-1760s.

The Younger Cochin
(left) Charles-Nicolas Cochin the Younger was a loyal friend to Chardin, and indefatigable in promoting his art. The year after Chardin died, he wrote an affectionate memoir of the artist, which to this day remains one of the prime sources of information about Chardin's character and working methods.

A print after Chardin
(above) The Elder Cochin was the first to make prints after two of Chardin's paintings in 1738, thus establishing a practice that led to a wide diffusion of Chardin's pictures. The two prints, including The Little Girl with Cherries (above), were advertised in the Mercure de France.

Portrait of the artist
(below left) The celebrated pastel portraitist, Maurice Quentin de La Tour, drew this portrait of Chardin in 1760. He prided himself on his ability to convey his sitter's personality, and the benevolent air he gives Chardin accords with Cochin's description of his friend's 'good sense and excellent judgement'.

efficiency, although his diligence never earned him the coveted post of Professor or Rector as these were reserved for history painters. The King began to buy more of his pictures – in 1751, he purchased one showing a lady with a musical box for the unusually large sum of 1500 livres, and in 1752, he granted Chardin a royal pension of 500 francs. Five years later Chardin was given the true seal of royal approval – lodgings in the Louvre.

Many of the royal dispensations that Chardin received in the 1750s and 1760s were in part due to the intervention of Charles-Nicolas Cochin, the son of the artist's engraver, who was also Secretary of the Academy. He was on very good terms with the Marquis de Marigny, Madame de Pompadour's brother, who after his appointment as Director General of Royal Buildings in 1754, was in a good position to hand out favours. Ever zealous on Chardin's behalf, Cochin solicited Marigny for increases in the artist's pension, and obtained commissions for decorative schemes for the royal chateaux of Choisy and Bellevue.

But Chardin's good fortune did not continue uninterrupted. There was the problem of his son Jean-Pierre, who was a constant source of

Les Attributs des Arts; Louvre, Paris

The Château de Choisy commission
(above and below) In 1764 Louis XV commissioned a decorative scheme for a salon in the Château de Choisy. Chardin painted this – Les Attributs des Arts *– and two similar pieces relating to music and science. The paintings were exhibited at the Salon (below), before being hung at the Château.*

son's education. Jean-Pierre signed a document renouncing his inheritance, and then revoked his decision, saying that he had been forced into it, and started legal proceedings against his father.

Neither side emerges well from this sordid story – neither the apparently tight-fisted father, nor the weak-willed and quarrelsome son. It is not known if good relations between them were ever restored, but on his way back from Rome in 1762 Jean-Pierre was kidnapped by pirates off the coast of Genoa, and disappeared for good. How he died remained a mystery, but the rumours that he later committed suicide in Venice only added to the ageing painter's grief.

Old age brought other problems, too. Chardin became increasingly plagued by pain from his gallstones, and his sight began to fail. The critics once again gave him unkind reviews, and accused him of endless repetition of the same subject. In the 1770s, Chardin's misfortunes increased when the Academy appointed a new Director, Jean-Baptiste Pierre, who was resolutely opposed both

disappointment to him. Although he had seemed all set to fulfil his father's ambitions by becoming a painter of history subjects, Jean-Pierre did not inherit the elder Chardin's remarkable talent. It was said at the time that he only won the coveted Prix de Rome – a competition open to art students – because the judges did not wish to upset his father. A strange altercation between father and son seems to have taken place before Jean-Pierre set off for Rome to take up the place he had won at the French school in 1754. The dispute involved the money left to Jean-Pierre by his mother, to which he was entitled on attaining his majority, and which Chardin tried to make him renounce on the grounds that it was due to him in payment for his

F. Jalain/Explorer

Louvre, Paris

Chardin's burial place
(above right) Chardin died in 1779 aged 80, and was buried in the Church of St Germain l'Auxerrois. His fortunes had declined considerably in the last few years of his life. At the time of his death, a new generation of French painters was beginning to make its presence felt, and the art-loving public no longer favoured Chardin's art, finding it outmoded and irrelevant. Seven of his paintings were sold with 15 items from his own collection, in an auction held the year after he died, and the potent charm of his work was to remain dormant until the middle of the following century.

to Cochin and Chardin himself. When, in 1774, the Marquis de Marigny was succeeded as Director General of Royal Buildings by the Comte d'Angiviller, who was ill-disposed towards Chardin, the artist's chances of procuring royal favours declined still further. His state pension was even reduced.

In an attempt to combat his waning popularity and his failing eyesight, Chardin turned to pastels in the last few years of his life. He exhibited several pastel studies of heads at the Salon in 1779 which met with some critical acclaim, but not the wholehearted enthusiasm that his work had attracted decades earlier. The critics were indulgent towards an 'indefatigable old man' and one of the pastels was even bought by a royal princess who sent Chardin a snuff box as a gift.

Notwithstanding this last success, Chardin's art had lost its popularity. Not until the mid-19th century, when the Goncourt brothers took up the cause of 18th-century French painting, and carefully examined Chardin's pictures for their painterly merits, did a reassessment emerge, and Chardin earn his true place as the most original painter of his generation.

A Labour of Love

The simplicity and harmony of Chardin's beautifully observed still-lifes and gentle genre pieces are the result of the artist's search for compositional perfection and his painstaking working method.

Chardin was the only major French artist of his generation who did not experience the rigorous training offered by the Academy. Although he came to lament his lack of formal art education, it was probably a blessing given the rigidity of the Academy's approach. In later life, Chardin spoke eloquently to the art-critic and philosopher Diderot about the sufferings of children who had pencils thrust into their hands at the age of seven or eight and were told to copy engravings or antique casts, and of the bitter tears of frustration they shed in front of statues of gladiators, goddesses and satyrs. Chardin himself never felt the need to look to the art of antiquity or the High Renaissance for his inspiration, and he found his early experience of copying engravings of classical statues in Cazes' studio desperately dull. Decades spent in this tedious pursuit would have undoubtedly stifled his gift for observation.

Chardin found the true direction of his talent the moment he realized that art did not have to be an artificial intellectual creation, but could be based on the everyday world he saw around him. The items he portrayed from his own kitchen and drawing room were selected for their formal qualities; their shapes, textures and colours, rather

The Water Urn (c.1734)
(right) Chardin began painting kitchen still-lifes in the early 1730s, choosing a limited number of ordinary household objects which were interesting for their shape and colour. This small work, painted in oil on wood, is one of the artist's most perfectly composed pictures. The copper urn was a favourite subject of Chardin's and reappears in the background of Girl Returning from Market *(p.61).*

Réunion des Musées Nationaux

Louvre, Paris

The Washerwoman (c.1733)
(right) One of Chardin's first genre scenes, this painting demonstrates the artist's sympathy for the activities of the middle-class household and the care he took with his composition.

The Schoolmistress (c.1735-6)
(left) Chardin simplified his later genre pieces, setting his figures against a plain background. In this charming painting Chardin concentrates on the subtle interaction between the subjects, conveying mood and unspoken exchanges not so much through facial expression as through the poses of the figures.

Nationalmuseum, Stockholm

National Gallery, London

than for any symbolic associations they may have had. In this respect, Chardin's art was fundamentally different from the work of painters of the Dutch school, with which it has often been compared. There is no sense in which his still lifes can be seen as *vanitas* works, or that his genre pieces illustrate a proverb or moral. They were simply painted to convey the visual pleasure that Chardin found in the objects of his own home.

TRANQUIL IMMOBILITY

Nor is there ever any sense of movement in his paintings to upset the studied equilibrium. Apart from the occasional dog eyeing a sideboard, or cat trying to snatch a morsel of food, most of the animals that Chardin painted were dead ones. His pictures showing the spoils of a day's shoot have none of the baroque exuberance that characterizes paintings of similar subjects by his contemporaries. The dead rabbits and birds are presented simply, lying on the kitchen table as the raw ingredients of a meal, rather than as a part of some legendary cornucopia. The people in Chardin's genre scenes are calm and poised and make no sudden gestures.

The genre pieces were successful – many of them were masterpieces of quiet perfection. In simple genre portraits like *The Schoolmistress* (opposite page) and in domestic interiors such as *Morning Toilet* (this page), Chardin portrays everyday incidents with an intimacy and directness which few other artists have ever achieved. But they cost Chardin a great deal of effort, and for the last 20 years of his life he devoted his time more and more to still-life painting. The critics of his time thought that Chardin had

National Galleries of Scotland, Edinburgh

Flowers in a Vase (c.1760-3)
(above) This simple still-life of white pinks, tuberoses and sweet peas is the only surviving painting of flowers by Chardin. The subject is treated in a surprisingly modern way, with wide brush strokes and thickly applied paint suggesting the petals of the flowers.

Morning Toilet (c. 1741)
(right) Chardin especially enjoyed painting women and children. In this intimate scene he captures marvellously the Sunday morning preparations for mass as a mother carefully arranges her daughter's hair, while the little girl watches in the mirror.

Nationalmuseum, Stockholm

51

exhausted his powers of invention, but the artist's originality lay not in a relentless search for new subjects, but in his mastery of technique. He enjoyed talking about the technical side of his craft with friends and colleagues, some of whom have left us detailed accounts of his working methods.

PAINTING FROM LIFE

According to these reports, Chardin always painted directly on to his canvas, working in front of the object rather than making elaborate sketches before he took up his paintbrush. Although he certainly did a number of drawings – indeed several portfolios of them were sold after his death – few that can be specifically related to his paintings have survived. This suggests that the artist found it easier to compose his pictures on the canvas itself. However, this did not necessarily make for a rapid method of work: Chardin worked slowly and laboriously, producing on average no more than two pictures per month. Each painting was the outcome of days of deliberation.

Chardin pursued a solitary path that set him apart from the artists of his time. What he was striving to achieve was a general effect. Right at the

Réunion des Musées Nationaux

COMPARISONS

Kitchen Scenes

Kitchen scenes first appeared in manuscript illuminations during the Middle Ages, but their popularity really blossomed in the 17th century. Part of their appeal was that they could be adapted for many purposes. For some artists – particularly those from Flanders – they offered the opportunity to paint still-lifes of abundant game and fruit. For others – especially the Dutch – lazy kitchen maids and profligate housewives provided an ideal vehicle for moral fable or ribald innuendo.

Nicolaes Maes (1634-93)
The Sleeping Kitchen Maid
(right) A pupil of Rembrandt, Nicolaes Maes was a Dutch genre and portrait painter, best known for the anecdotal scenes of Dutch interiors which he painted in the 1650s.

National Gallery, London

Pieter Aertsen (1508-1575)
Christ in the House of Martha and Mary
(left) A Dutch painter who spent much of his working life in Flanders, Pieter Aertsen produced monumental works, often on a religious theme, set in a kitchen or a butcher's shop. Here the biblical content is relegated to the background, while the foreground is dominated by a colourful still-life of meat, fruit and vegetables in the Flemish tradition.

Archiv für Kunst und Geschichte

Christ with Mary and Martha/Museum Boymans van Beuningen, Rotterdam

The Jar of Olives (1760)
*(left) One of the largest
and most ambitious of
Chardin's late still-lifes,
this painting shows the
artist's skill in conveying
light and atmosphere. The
soft light is reflected in the
glasses and gives the wine
a naturalistic
transparency, while the
olives appear to float in the
water in their tall glass
jar. The Meissen porcelain
(detail below) is
particularly well
portrayed, its smooth,
hard surface contrasting
with the textures of the
soft fruit and paté (far left).*

Louvre, Paris

outset of his career he told a friend: 'I must forget
what I have seen and even the way in which these
objects have been treated by others. I must set
myself at a distance so that I do not see the details.
I must particularly try to imitate, as truthfully as
possible, general masses, tones and colour,
roundness, effects of light and shade.' Detail was
not important to Chardin – it was usually lost in his
thickly applied impasto – what mattered was the
arrangement of objects within the picture space.

A PERFECT BALANCE

Another important aspect of Chardin's art was
his harmonious use of colour and tone. After
priming his canvas, Chardin applied a thin coat of
oil colour (generally a mixture of white lead and a
reddish-brown pigment) which gave him a fairly
dark background on to which he could place the
dark areas, then the half tones, and finally the
highlights. When he had arrived at the right tonal
balance, he added colour, balancing each area of
bright colour with a correspondingly dark area.
After finishing the picture, Chardin went over it
again with the colours he had already used in
order to harmonize it.

Items in the painting were linked together by
touches of colour that related each subject to its
neighbours – the red of a flower or a strawberry,
for example, would always be echoed somewhere
else in the picture. These careful efforts conspired
to create a pleasing and apparently naturalistic
effect. As Chardin's friend, Diderot, put it: 'To look
at pictures by other artists, it seems that I need to
borrow a different pair of eyes. To look at those of
Chardin, I have only to keep the eyes Nature gave
me and make good use of them.'

53

THE MAKING OF A MASTERPIECE

Saying Grace

On 27 November 1740, Philibert Orry, the Minister of Culture, introduced Chardin to Louis XV. The artist presented the King with two pendant paintings he had shown that year at the Salon, *The Diligent Mother* (p.62), and *Saying Grace*, and the King liked them so much that he placed them in his study. The pictures did not reappear in public until 1845, when they were exhibited in the Louvre. *Saying Grace* soon became one of the museum's most popular masterpieces. The subject was a favourite with Dutch 17th-century artists, but they often emphasized its religious significance. Chardin presented it simply as an episode of everyday life, delicately conveying a mood of intimacy in the triangle of looks exchanged between the mother and her children as they prepare to eat their modest meal.

Louvre, Paris

Réunion des Musées Nationaux

A sketch of a lost original
(above) *Chardin painted several versions of his most popular works, and he allowed copies to be made of* The Diligent Mother *and* Saying Grace. *This drawing by Saint-Aubin in his catalogue of the 1761 Salon records a composition by Chardin which is clearly a variant of the earlier* Saying Grace. *The painting is now thought to be lost, although a copy (right) – still considered by some scholars to be an original – exists in Rotterdam.*

Museum Boymans-van Beuningen

The Rotterdam painting
(left) *This composition is similar to that sketched by Saint-Aubin, although the painting is generally thought to be a copy. It is unlikely that it is an original – despite the disparaging remarks made by Diderot about the quality of Chardin's 1761 painting – because of its rather poor finish.*

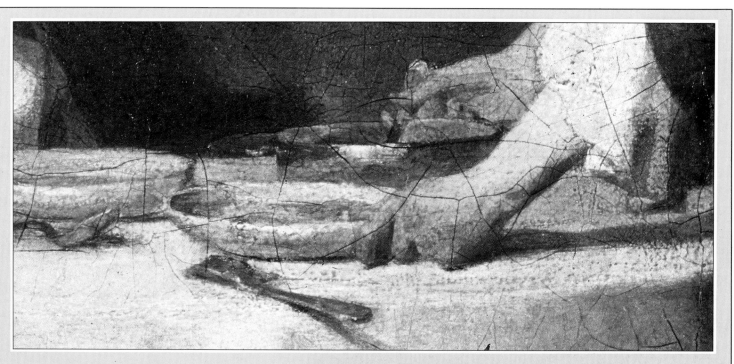

Humble fare

(above) The young mother carefully serves out the meal she has prepared, and Chardin gently contrasts the redness of her hands – sore from hard work – with the unsoiled white of her muslin sleeves.

Childhood innocence

(right) The picture derives its French name – 'Le Bénédicté – from the first word of the grace uttered by the little child before the family begins its meal.

Kitchen objects

(below) This beautifully painted still-life detail shows a small pot filled with charcoal which was used to warm or reheat the meal.

Gallery

Chardin began his career painting still-lifes of kitchen utensils, fish, meat and vegetables, such as Kitchen Still-Life with Cooking Pots and Eggs. Critics soon recognized his remarkable talent for composing pictures of balance and serenity, and these unpretentious works enjoyed popularity for well over a decade.

Kitchen Still-Life with Cooking Pots and Eggs *c.1734*
6½″ × 8″ Louvre, Paris

The apparent simplicity of this still-life, composed from the objects in Chardin's kitchen, belies the careful deliberation that went into its creation. The light stone surface of the table and the neutral background act as foils for the rich copper of the pot and the creamy whiteness of the eggs. The diagonal line formed by the leek offsets the insistent horizontal of the table edge.

In the late 1730s, however, Chardin turned to figure painting, producing simple genre scenes which included half-length portraits like The Young Draughtsman and domestic interiors such as The Governess and The Diligent Mother. He always kept to what he knew he could do best, capturing the quiet moments of a household rather than attempting to portray violent emotion or movement, and painting everyday objects with as much care as the characters.

As he exhausted the possibilities of genre painting, Chardin returned to still-life in the 1750s, showing a new fluidity of touch and exuberance of colour in works like The Cut Melon and Grapes and Pomegranates.

Bulloz

Kitchen Still-Life with Pestle and Mortar *c.1734*
6½″ × 8″ Musée Cognacq-Jay, Paris

This picture may well have been a pendant to the painting opposite as it is clearly related in composition, but contains subtle differences that produce witty variations on the same theme. A pestle and mortar replaces the pepper pot, onions appear instead of eggs, a knife instead of a leek protrudes over the edge of the table and the copper cooking pot is turned on its side.

Little Girl with a Shuttlecock *1737*
31¾″ × 24¾″ Private Collection, Paris

This charming painting once belonged to Catherine the Great, the Empress of Russia. Attempts have been made to read the picture as an allegory, with the racket and shuttlecock representing the transience of pleasure. However, it is more likely that it simply records a game that was very popular among children at the time.

The Young Draughtsman 1737
31½″ × 25½″ Louvre, Paris

*Chardin's strong feelings on the shortcomings of art education gave
this popular subject a particularly personal relevance. A boy sharpens
his chalk stick before continuing his work: it is difficult to tell whether
the drawing is a caricature of an old man or the type of study
Chardin deplored – a drawing after an antique statue.*

The Governess *1738*
18½″ × 14¾″ National Gallery of Canada, Ottawa

A governess is brushing the young boy's hat before he sets off for school. The lovingly portrayed objects on the floor amplify the implied narrative: an open sewing-basket suggests the woman's industriousness, while the cards, racket and shuttlecock represent the childish pleasures the boy must leave behind.

Girl Returning from Market *1739*
18½″ × 15″ Louvre, Paris

A girl has just come back from shopping bearing a leg of mutton and loaves of bread. Chardin embellishes this simple scene by including a further vignette of domestic life glimpsed through an open door, and he unifies the painting by echoing the foreground shades of blue, rose, cream and brown in the room in the background.

Bulloz

The Diligent Mother *1740*
19″ × 15″ Louvre, Paris

As a mother examines a piece of embroidery with her daughter, an unspoken dialogue seems to pass between the two figures. Small details such as the candle slightly askew in its holder, the teapot and cup on the mantlepiece, and the scissors dangling from the woman's waist give the scene an air of authenticity.

Saying Grace 1740
19″ × 15″ Louvre, Paris

*This is probably Chardin's best-known painting. It was acclaimed
during his own lifetime as a parable on the womanly virtues of order,
calm and piety, and compared to the fables of La Fontaine. The
expression of the little girl watching the younger child's faltering
attempts at saying grace is particularly well observed.*

The Jar of Apricots *1758*
22″ × 20″ Art Gallery of Ontario, Toronto

In the 1750s, when Chardin once again turned his attention to still-life painting, he simplified the detail of his earlier work and began to lay on paint in smoother, broader areas. Here this approach succeeds in conveying a marvellous impression of the apricots glistening in their jar, and the gleam of light upon glass and china.

The Cut Melon *1760*
22″ × 20″ Private Collection, Paris

Detailed examination of this picture reveals how Chardin balanced the tones and colours in his paintings as carefully as he arranged the elements of line and mass. The acid orange of the melon is set against the soft warm red of the peaches, and both these vibrant tones are seen to advantage beside the dull greens of the bottles and leaves.

Grapes and Pomegranates *1763*
18½″ × 22¼″ Louvre, Paris

In several of Chardin's late still-lifes the humble kitchen utensils of his early work have been replaced with luscious assemblies of fruit and porcelain. It is easy to see that the china came from Chardin's own drawing room, as the same items tend to recur in different pictures. The decorated water jug that appears in **The Cut Melon** *(p.2231) is seen here from a slightly different angle. More unusual in Chardin's work are the exotic pomegranates.*

Réunion des Musées Nationaux

The Brioche *1763*
18½″ × 22″ Louvre, Paris

*This picture and its pendant opposite were almost certainly among
the six still-lifes which met with enormous critical acclaim when they
were exhibited at the Salon of 1763. It was the artist's ability to
render in a convincing yet simple manner the contrasting textures of
objects such as the soft crust of the brioche and the shiny hardness of
the Meissen bowl that led Diderot to exclaim that Chardin worked not
with paint, but with the very essence of the objects themselves.*

Life Below Stairs

In Chardin's time, more than a million and a half French men and women worked out their lives in domestic service, living 'below stairs' in the houses of the aristocracy and the bourgeoisie.

Hunterian Art Gallery, University of Glasgow

At the time Chardin was painting his celebrated pictures of life below stairs in the 1730s, Paris was almost overflowing with servants. All day long, the streets near Chardin's home in the Rue Princesse would echo to the sounds of footmen and other servants hastening about their business.

Each aristocratic household – and many belonging to the rising middle classes too – had its own retinue of servants or *domestiques*. Many houses had more than 30; some had over 200. Even Chardin himself, despite his financial problems, had Marie-Anne Cheneau, the model for many of his paintings.

Though many servants in smaller households were, like Marie-Anne, simply maids-of-all-work, the big houses had innumerable kinds of different servants. There were *valets des chambres* to attend to their master's every whim; stewards to run the affairs of the house; butlers to look after the wine and silver; chambermaids (*chambrières*) to attend the ladies of the house; young lackeys (or *jacquets*)

to perform menial tasks; cooks and kitchen maids to prepare the dinner and clean up; coachmen, grooms, chairmen, laundry maids, postillions and many more besides.

As a rule, there was a rigid hierarchy of 'upper' and 'lower' servants and each servant had his or her own duties and status. At the top of the tree was the steward, an impressive figure who managed the house and was often treated as an equal by the master. At the bottom was the scullery maid who was, at best, ignored.

DIVIDED LIVES

Upper servants, such as the steward, the valet and the lady's maid, were invariably highly trained and their conditions reflected their elevated status. While lower menservants, notably *jacquets*, were expected to wear *la livrée* (brightly coloured livery and gold braid), upper servants were generally allowed to wear ordinary clothes. Similarly, while kitchen maids wore coarse woollen clothes, lady's maids usually dressed in their mistress's cast-off silks and satins.

Giraudon

The servant at work *(above left) Abandoning the stately or epic subject matter favoured by many of his contemporaries, Chardin excelled in his paintings of domestic life. Several of his paintings show servants engaged in some familiar daily task – cleaning the pans, gathering up bread, or, as in this painting of* The Cellar Boy, *preparing the jugs which are to be used in filling the wine bottles for the table.*

H. Roger Viollet

Turkish Woman and her slave/Museum of Art and History, Geneva

Oriental elegance
(left) To enhance their mistress's status, maidservants were often encouraged to follow the fashion of the day. Chardin's Swiss contemporary, Jean-Etienne Liotard, painted this unusual portrait of a French lady and her maid soon after his return from Constantinople. The exotic silks and stilted shoes of the Turkish costume create a romantic grandeur, while literally elevating the mistress to a higher level.

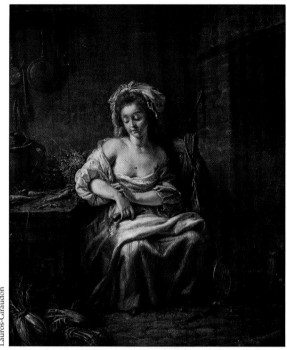

Lauros-Giraudon

P. Moitte; The Kitchenmaid/Musée Picardie, Amiens

Upper and lower servants always ate and slept separately. Upper servants ate well in their own rooms, often dining off the same food that they fed their masters – when they were dining-off the left-overs, unwary guests pausing for a moment while eating would frequently find full plates whisked away from under their noses. Lower servants, however, would eat in the servants' hall or the kitchen, feeding on the upper servants' left-overs.

For many upper servants, life was relatively comfortable. A valet, for instance, might find that once he had dressed his master in the morning he was left with the entire day to himself, while a lady's maid might be treated as a friend and confidante of her mistress. For the poor lower servant, however, work was invariably arduous. A young scullery maid, for instance, had to crawl

Kitchen morals
(above) Often alone in the city, women servants were vulnerable to the advances of both master and servant. In this painting, the kitchen maid is presented as a woman of 'loose morals' – a common notion in the 18th century, strengthened by the unfortunate connection between prostitution and domestic service.

The patisserie
(left) Below stairs' life always centred on the kitchen which, in many large 18th-century households, would also include a patisserie. On the right-hand side of this engraving, the cook can be seen carefully checking the day's produce.

The picnic
(right) It was in the 18th-century that picnicking first became fashionable. Even on picnics an array of footmen was required to serve the food and to tend the horses.

Telaric/Giraudon

The Hunt Luncheon; Carle van Loo/Louvre, Paris

Lauros-Giraudon

A Lunch of Oysters; J. F. de Troy/Musée Condé, Chantilly

Explorer Archives

Oyster feast

(left) A rowdy dinner of oysters and champagne could provide its own feast of leftovers for the wily servant. In this colourful painting by François de Troy, the attention of the guests is distracted by a champagne cork which can be seen flying through the air.

Lord of the carriage

(below) If a clerk of the stables was employed, the job of the coachman was restricted to mere driving, but otherwise he was a figure of some authority – controlling grooms, postillions and stable hands and having overall responsibility for the care of the horses.

from her cold attic bed at five in the morning to clean the kitchen range and light the ovens. All day long, she scoured pots and scrubbed floors with barely a moment's rest. It might be one in the morning before she could climb back to bed.

Of course, some masters treated their servants fairly well. Few thought of doing without them – most believing, like the English historian Edward Gibbon, there was nothing to match 'the indispensable comfort of a servant'. But there was no shortage of books of advice on how to get the best from your servants, by churchmen such as Fenelon and Claude Fleury, and aristocrats such as the Prince de Comty – there was even one, *La Maison Reglée* (The Ordered House), by a steward, Jean Audiger.

All these books emphasized that servants owed their master total obedience in exchange for their food and clothing. But they also emphasized that the master had a duty to act as moral guardian to his servants. According to Fleury, a master 'must consider it inevitable that every [servant] has a fault and must charitably endeavour to correct it'. Just as the servant owed it to a master 'to suffer, to work and to be silent', so a master owed his servants 'bread, work and punishment'.

Over the course of the century, this 'paternalistic' attitude tended to give way to a more business-like arrangement, especially

Bridgeman Art Library

View of Potrel Manor-J. Griffier/Roy Miles Gallery

70

The Lady's maid
*(right and left) The job of
the maidservant was
skilled and often very
demanding. It was she
who had to wake her
mistress in the morning
and prepare her hair and
dress for the day ahead.
But as she would
sometimes serve as
companion at home and in
public, she had to be
educated in the arts of
social, as well as domestic,
finesse.*

The learned domestic
*(below right) Teaching
servants to read and write
was not always done from
a charitable impulse.
Often, as shown in this
painting by Hubert
Robert, an educated
servant could fulfil the
practical function of
reading aloud to his
employer during dinner.*

La Chocolatiere; J. F. Liotard/Stäatliche Museum, Dresden

as domestic servants since they were uncorrupted by the 'vices' of the city — so popular, indeed, that out-of-work servants could improve their chances of employment by walking out into the country and joining the wagon-loads of young country people rolling into the city every day.

Many of these countrymen were fleeing the lottery for army service — a good master could use his influence to save his servants from the draft. Many were escaping feudal ties. Others were driven by sheer poverty. And some were simply drawn by the bright lights of Paris.

For some countrywomen, though, there was no alternative if they were not to lead a life of prostitution — and many naïve girls new to Paris were lured into this life anyway. Countrywomen, unlike their urban counterparts, had to marry to secure their future. Yet few peasant families could afford a dowry, particularly if one or both parents died young, as many did. Domestic service in the city was one of the few ways open to these women to scrimp and save a dowry for themselves.

It might take eight or nine years to save their dowry and escape domestic service, but many women had their hopes dashed — often because the comparatively poor wages that womenservants received meant that they had to lower their expectations for a husband. As one *chambrière* lamented to her friend after many years servitude, 'Now for our money, the best we can get is a coachman or a stableboy, who will make three or four children in a row. And since they cannot feed them on the paltry wages they earn, we have to go back and serve as before.'

among the bourgeoisie. But if the benevolent master regarded his servants as children, few servants thought of him as their father. They were, after all, in his house through necessity, rather than through any choice of their own.

SERVING FOR GAIN

When Molière's Don Juan is dragged down into hell, in the 17th-century play of the same name, his manservant Sganarelle's only comment is to cry 'My wages, my wages'. Though the play is satirical, Sganarelle's 'callousness' reflects a wide-felt attitude among servants. Legrain, valet to one of the heroes of the French revolution, Count Mirabeau, for more than 30 years, had a similarly pragmatic attitude to his master's death. After leaving his tired and pregnant wife to tend to the count in his last moments, Legrain explained, 'He had not forgotten us but, where there is nothing, the king himself loses his rights'. It may be this attitude among valets, one of the few kinds of servants with a real chance of betterment, that led to the tradition of wily servants in French literature, such as Figaro in Beaumarchais' play *The Barber of Seville*.

It may be the hope of betterment that brought so many country people to Paris to work as domestic servants. Country people were popular

In a year when Chardin was creating the quiet, masterly pastels of his old age, an era of upheavals was foreshadowed in both politics and the arts. In America, hostilities flared into what became the War of Independence, while in Europe early stirrings of romanticism and revolution were in the air.

In 1775, after ten years of rising tension, the Thirteen Colonies broke into open revolt against George III and his government. Having already closed the port of Boston and restricted many traditional American rights, the British government prepared for still harsher measures.

One such measure was an expedition mounted in secrecy and sent out from Boston to nearby Concord to seize a suspected stockpile of arms and ammunition. Boston 'patriots' heard of the raid, and express riders (the most famous being Paul Revere) raised the countryside. At a confrontation between troops and colonial militiamen on the green at Lexington, a gun went off, perhaps accidentally, and eight Americans were killed. The British completed their mission at Concord, but were harassed unmercifully by sharpshooters all

Royal coronation
(below) Louis XVI had become King of France in 1774 on the death of his grandfather, Louis XV. His reign, sanctified by his coronation the following year, was to be haunted by revolution, at home and abroad.

AISA

A new life
(right) By 1775 the 26-year-old Johann Wolfgang von Goethe had already made his name as a poet, dramatist and novelist in the forefront of the new 'Storm and Stress' school, but its emphasis on emotion over convention and order brought Goethe to the edge of an artistic crisis. However, a chance invitation by the Grand Duke in November led to a visit to Weimar which was to be Goethe's home until his death in 1832. His increasing role in the running of the little duchy acted as a stabilizing influence preparatory to the Italian journey (1786-88) which so influenced his life and work.

Goethe Museum, Frankfurt

Bildarchiv Preussischer Kulturbesitz

The Battle of Bunker Hill
(above and right) By spring 1775, the American colonists had built up a substantial Patriot militia and were preparing for war. The British governor, General Gage, was urged to restore Royal Authority, but the rebel militia responded to the bloody skirmishes of Lexington and Concord by surrounding Boston and thus bottling up the British forces. On 16 June, 3000 patriots foiled Gage's plan to occupy Charlestown Heights by making entrenchments on the peninsula themselves. British ships on the Charles River began shelling at dawn and by early afternoon the infantry had crossed over. It took three advances before they succeeded in capturing Breeds Hill, causing the rebel army to retreat to Bunker Hill and then across Charlestown Neck. Despite victory, the siege of Boston continued until the British army was evacuated the following March.

the way back to Boston and suffered almost 300 casualties.

After this, events moved swiftly. Rebel forces surrounded and besieged Boston. At a 'Continental Congress' in May, the colonies created the nucleus of a Continental Army, commanded by a prominent Virginian named George Washington. Meanwhile, rebels led by Ethan Allen captured Fort Ticonderoga, and with it 200 British field guns. In June, when the British attempted to take Bunker Hill overlooking Boston, they were mown down as they charged again and again. The Redcoats were eventually victorious but at a cost of almost half of a force of 2,200 men. The colonists then marched north to carry the war into Canada, and only winter, an energetic defence and the threat of British reinforcements, saved Quebec the following year.

The theatrical successes of 1775 were varied. Richard Brinsley Sheridan's *The Rivals* failed when it was put on at Covent Garden in January, but was acclaimed later in the year after being recast and partly rewritten. In Paris, a comedy became an important instrument of subversion in the hands of Beaumarchais, whose *Barber of Seville* covertly poked fun at the privileged and futile aristocratic way of life. The *Barber* and the later *Marriage of Figaro* became two of the landmarks on the road to revolution.

The Romantic movement had already appeared in central Europe with the 'Storm and Stress' school of writers with which Johann Wolfgang von Goethe, Germany's greatest man of letters, was deeply associated. However, by 1775, the year in which he settled at Weimar, Goethe had begun to turn towards

Scots inventor
(below) In 1775, James Watt and his partner Matthew Boulton successfully applied to prolong the term of Watt's patent for a condensing steam engine by 25 years. Watt's invention had grafted a condenser onto Newcomen's engine, thus creating a more economical machine. By 1783, the firm of Boulton and Watt had replaced all but of Newcomen's pumping engines in Cornwall. Later models were adapted to drive all kinds of machinery with the result that Watt's engines could truly be said to have powered the Industrial Revolution.

Giancarlo Costa

National Portrait Gallery, London

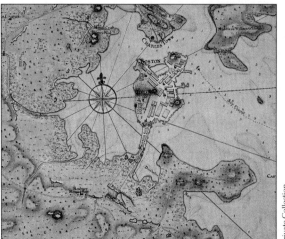

Private Collection

Bridgeman Art Library

the more moderating influence of classicism, gradually evolving his personal philosophy of fulfilment and the attainment of individual freedom through selfless activity.

RUSSIAN ABSOLUTISM UNDER THREAT

In Russia, the prospect of freedom for any group except the nobility was fading fast. Although the Empress Catherine, German by birth, liked to present herself as an 'enlightened despot' and sponsored a few token reforms, her policies always favoured the nobility at the expense of the peasants, for whom the burden of serfdom became ever heavier. In 1775, there were new reforms which tightened the provincial administration, but these were produced by fear rather than enlightenment.

The great peasant revolt of 1773-4, led by Emelyan Pugachov, had seriously threatened Catherine's position. Pugachov, a Don Cossack, had raised the disaffected peasants by the traditional Russian method of imposture: he claimed to be the Tsar Peter III, Catherine's erstwhile husband, who had been eliminated in 1762. Pugachov's was the most successful of all Russian peasant revolts, uniting serfs, Cossacks and religious dissidents, as it spread over a vast area east of the Volga. Many landowners were murdered and all but the most important towns fell to the rebels. Only when peace with Turkey released the Russian army did the government regain control. Eventually Pugachov was captured and brought to Moscow. Given a mock 'coronation' with a red-hot crown, Pugachov was executed in January 1775.

C. Masson/Kipa

The Barber of Seville
(above) Pierre Augustin Caron Beaumarchais' celebrated comedy The Barber of Seville was first performed on 23 February 1775 to immediate acclaim. Based on his own experiences in Madrid as agent to a Parisian financier, the story revolves around the central character of Figaro, a barber of immense resource, optimism and impudence who succeeds in confounding all obstacles to his friend Count Almaviva's marriage to the beautiful Rosina – to his own profit, of course. Both The Barber of Seville and its more politically orientated sequel The Marriage of Figaro (1784) are better known today through the operatic works of Rossini and Mozart respectively.

Bridgeman Art Library

Prado, Madrid

Charles III of Spain
(left) Charles III (1726-88) was an enlightened absolutist monarch whose internal reforms created a Spanish cultural and economic revival. The King was not so fortunate with his foreign policy. Spain's decision in 1775 to back the rebel colonists in the Americas involved her in a costly war with the English, and the Spanish attack of the same year on the pirate stronghold of Algiers proved disastrous.

Portrait of Boucher: Gustav Lundberg/Réunion des Musées Nationaux

f Boucher

1703 – 1770

François Boucher, the greatest decorative painter to emerge in 18th century France, was born in Paris in 1703. He grew up during the sparkling years of the Regency when masked balls and café society made their return to the capital. After a brief spell of study with Lemoyne, he found work as an engraver. In 1723, he won the Prix de Rome which enabled him to spend three years studying in Italy, visiting Venice, Parma and Rome.

On his return to Paris, Boucher was accepted into the Academy and embarked on a dazzling career. His versatility brought him commissions for tapestries, stage scenery and porcelain designs, and to all these he brought his blend of casual elegance and playful eroticism. Through his influential patron, Madame de Pompadour, he achieved the greatest artistic honours in France, just 20 years before the Revolution.

The Pleasure-loving Parisian

A lively, amorous man with an extremely generous nature, Boucher was the favourite artist of the King's mistress, Madame de Pompadour, and the greatest decorative painter of his day.

In September 1703, François Boucher was born in the Rue de la Verrerie, in the eleventh district of Paris. His father, Nicolas, was a painter and designer of modest talents, who earned his living by selling prints and artists' materials.

François was raised in the rooms above his father's shop and must have been involved in the work of the family business from an early age. This in itself provided the boy with a broad-based artistic training for, in addition to his prints and paintings, Nicolas also produced book illustrations and designs for decorative schemes. François inherited this versatility and exploited it to the full.

Boucher's father realized, however, the need to entrust the completion of his son's education to the care of a more skilled artist and thus, at the age of seventeen, François entered the studio of François Lemoyne. This was an auspicious move as Lemoyne was very much a rising star and led the way in promoting a more decorative form of the Baroque, culminating in the Rococo style at which

Lemoyne's Venus and Adonis

(right) At the age of 17, Boucher entered the studio of François Lemoyne, an established painter with an exuberant, colourful style. Boucher claimed that he learned little from him, but a few of their works are indistinguishable.

Parisian upbringing

(below) Boucher was born in Paris in September 1703, in the area around the Louvre. His father ran a small but successful print shop and the family lived in the rooms above.

his teenaged pupil was later to excel.

With characteristic flippancy, Boucher later asserted that Lemoyne was a poor teacher and it is true that he remained in the master's studio for only a few months. However, in that time, he managed to absorb many of the most important features of Lemoyne's style – in particular, his taste for stressing the decorative rather than the narrative aspect of his mythological subjects, and the warmth and vibrancy of his flesh tones.

Boucher found work immediately, joining the workshop of Jean-François Cars, the father of one of his friends. Cars ran a flourishing engraving business and the young artist was soon engaged on a wide variety of tasks, designing frontispieces, armorial crests and communion cards. Once again, this experience was to prove invaluable.

Through his work at Cars' studio, Boucher gained his first important commission. A friend of Antoine Watteau, Jean de Julienne, was so impressed with his technical ability that he hired

Boutin/Explorer

Nationalmuseum, Stockholm

The lessons of Watteau
(above) Boucher's first major commission was to engrave 125 of Watteau's drawings, which had been collected together in a two volume work entitled Figures de Différents Caractères. *Watteau's superb draughtsmanship had a distinct influence on Boucher's drawing style, seen especially in his studies of women.*

Boucher to assist in the engraving of 125 of Watteau's best-known drawings. The work for Cars and Julienne did not cause Boucher to neglect his painting however. In 1723, he won the much-coveted Prix de Rome, a signal honour which carried with it enrolment for a course of study at the French Academy in Rome.

A DELAYED DEPARTURE

In the event, Boucher did not travel to Italy until 1727. The delay may have been due to a lack of funds – at this stage, the Academy could not always afford to finance the trip and a private patron had to be found – or it may simply have been a mark of reluctance on the part of the artist to leave his home because he was revelling in Paris life and earning himself quite a reputation.

Nevertheless, an educational tour of Italy was still essential for the career prospects of any aspiring artist and so Boucher travelled south, in the company of Carle van Loo and his two nephews. Information about his stay there is limited and has been coloured by the painter's own disparaging remarks. Boucher later commented that he went to Italy more out of curiosity than out of genuine interest.

Even so, there is some evidence to suggest that, while staying in his 'little hole of a room' in Rome, he came to appreciate the works of Francesco Albani and Pietro da Cortona, and also that,

Roman trip
(above) In 1723 Boucher won the Prix de Rome and in 1727 he travelled south to Italy. During his stay in Rome he was most impressed by the Baroque masters.

The youthful master
(below) This fanciful self-portrait shows the young Boucher, surrounded by the paraphernalia of his studio, painting an Italianate landscape.

during his visit to Venice, he may have come into contact with the great decorative artist, Tiepolo.

By 1731, Boucher was back in Paris, working to gain admittance to the Academy. Within three years, he had achieved this when his *Rinaldo and Armida* (below right) was accepted as his 'morceau de réception' (entry piece). This painting offered clear indicators to Boucher's future development. The subject was drawn from the classics – as was to be expected from a prospective Academician – but Boucher paid only lip-service to his source, using it as a pretext for his unashamed glorification of naked female flesh.

Boucher had already found his chief model by this time. In 1733, he married seventeen-year old Marie-Jeanne Buseau in Paris. Boucher's pretty young wife was to become the prototype for the nubile nymphs and goddesses personified in his many depictions of Venus, Diana and Leda. Ironically, though, one of his most charming depictions of the lady shows her fully-clothed, on a sofa, in a witty display of domestic intimacy.

Boucher was incapable of remaining faithful to his wife for long and soon continued with his succession of brief, casual affairs. However, his infidelities were never protracted or serious and they did not endanger his marriage – principally because Marie-Jeanne enjoyed liaisons of her own. The couple had two daughters and a son and always stayed on friendly terms, even though, in later life, Boucher found his wife's extravagance something of a strain on their finances.

Marie-Jeanne was a painter in her own right, executing competent miniature copies of her husband's work. François' career, meanwhile, was going from strength to strength. In 1735 – long before his association with Madame de Pompadour – he received his first royal commission, providing panels of the Virtues for Marie Leczinska, Louis XV's frumpish wife.

DECORATIVE PROJECTS

In the year before, Boucher began producing designs for the tapestry factory at Beauvais, working under the directorship of Jean-Baptiste Oudry. This was only one aspect of his lifelong connection with the applied arts. From 1737, he also found employment with the Opéra. The theatre had always been one of his passions and he

Mme Boucher
(right) In 1733, having tired of his bachelor existence, Boucher, married Marie-Jeanne Buseau.

Marie's admirer
(far right) While Boucher continued to have casual affairs, his wife enjoyed a brief liaison with the Swedish Ambassador, Tessin. Tessin was so entranced by the delicate Marie that he commissioned many works from Boucher as an excuse to see her.

Rinaldo and Armida
(below) This was Boucher's entrance piece to the Academy.

Decorative Works

Boucher's work as a decorative artist led him to produce designs for an astonishing variety of objects, including clocks, fountains and puppets, in addition to tapestries and porcelain. For the Gobelins and Beauvais tapestry factories he produced mythologies, exotic chinoiseries and delightful pastorals, while for the porcelain works at Sèvres – a pet project of Mme de Pompadour – he executed a series of charming infants.

The Music Lesson/Victoria and Albert Museum

Petit Palais, Paris

Réunion des Musées Nationaux

Porcelain figures
(left) Boucher's designs for the Sèvres porcelain factory proved so popular that the traditional supremacy of the Meissen porcelain works was threatened.

Beauvais tapestry
(above) The Beauvais tapestries were executed to Boucher's designs. The artist's style was a perfect reflection of urban taste.

Boucher/Portrait of Madame Boucher/The Frick Collection, New York

Jacques Aved/Portrait of C.G. Tessin/Nationalmuseum, Stockholm

Louvre, Paris

threw himself energetically into the task of painting stage scenery and designing costumes.

1737 was also the year in which the Salon re-opened its doors on an annual basis after a long closure. Boucher's main contribution was a set of pastorals representing the Four Seasons, which were universally acclaimed and which unleashed a flow of commissions. Sadly, his old teacher did not live to witness this moment of triumph. Burdened with overwork and grief-stricken at the loss of his wife, Lemoyne had committed suicide two months earlier.

The next two decades proved a period of almost uninterrupted success for Boucher. His work – be it paintings, tapestries or interior decoration – was constantly in demand from aristocratic and royal patrons alike. Of the latter, the most influential by far was Madame de Pompadour. Once installed as Louis XV's official mistress, in 1745, she lost no time in involving Boucher in the plethora of artistic projects which she initiated.

The most dazzling of Boucher's work for Madame de Pompadour must have been the decorations for her château at Bellevue – now sadly destroyed. Boucher produced chinoiserie designs for her boudoir, light-hearted mythological scenes for her bedroom and even a rare religious panel for her chapel. The full scope of his talents was tested. When his patroness set up a private theatre for the King's amusement, Boucher was called upon to provide the scenery; when she took an interest in the revitalized porcelain industry, he was commissioned to execute the drawings for a collection of soft paste biscuit figures.

The most notable of Boucher's surviving works for his distinguished patroness is a marvellous series of portraits. Here, Boucher's art reached the peak of its refinement, as Madame de Pompadour

Bulloz

Boucher's daughter
(left) In 1758 Boucher celebrated the double wedding of his daughters to his gifted pupils, Baudouin and Deshayes. He painted this portrait of the new Mme Baudoin a few years into her marriage.

Decorated apartments
(below) At the height of his career Boucher received many royal commissions for decorative schemes. The Salle du Conseil at Fontainebleau (1753) is one of the few that has survived intact.

Denis Diderot (1713-84)

A leading philosopher and editor of the great 'Encyclopedia' (1751-72), Diderot was also a pioneering art critic. As such, he expressed a growing dissatisfaction with the frivolous decay which he found in both the society and painting of the Ancien Régime. For Diderot, visual splendour was not enough; art had to display a rational or emotional power. Thus, in his vituperative Salon reviews, he deplored Boucher's moral redundancy and his apparent uninterest in the workings of nature. In 1765 he made his most personal attack on Boucher, declaring that he was responsible for 'the degradation of taste' and the 'depravation of morals'.

The dedicated journalist
(right) This portrait of Diderot by Louis-Michel van Loo conveys the witty, incisive nature of Diderot's writing, showing the great critic poised in the act of penning his thoughts.

Musée Cognacq-Jay, Paris

posed elegantly amid a profusion of flowers, with her books and her music by her side. Not that this image was always greeted with enthusiasm. At the Salon of 1757, a storm of protest arose when some papers depicted by her bedside were interpreted as ministerial documents, thereby fuelling the suspicion that she was running the country.

A SWEDISH PATRON

Boucher, however, did not work exclusively for the Court. Prominent among his many other patrons was Count Tessin, the Swedish ambassador. Tessin's attraction to the artist's work is said to have been reinforced by his attraction to Boucher's wife and, certainly, the gifts he lavished upon her were frequently more costly than the paintings he purchased. Boucher remained indulgent, though, and was even content to portray Marie-Jeanne as a naked goddess in the Count's *Triumph of Venus* (pp.88-9).

In 1752, Boucher achieved a long-cherished ambition when he was granted the use of a studio in the Louvre. He was now at the peak of his career, commanding high fees and with a volume of work that compelled him to use assistants.

Boucher's favourite students were, by and large, a disappointment to him. His son trained as an architect but was without talent and his two sons-in-law, Baudouin and Deshays, both died young before their true potential could be fulfilled. The spirit of his work survived, to an extent, in the output of another of his assistants, Jean-Honoré Fragonard, but the most famous painter to pass through his workshop was to pioneer a very different style. The young David, a distant relative of Boucher's, trained only briefly with him before moving on to formulate his astringent, classical

Réunion des Musées Nationaux

Louvre, Paris

Hubert Robert/View of the Grande Galerie in the Louvre/Louvre, Paris

Carle van Loo

(below) Carle van Loo was an old friend of Boucher and the most eminent artist of his day. When he died in 1765 Boucher was chosen to fill his position as Chief Court Painter and Director of the Academy.

Death in the Louvre

(above) In 1752 Boucher had been granted the use of a studio in the Louvre. He died there in May 1770; there is a romantic story, probably apocryphal, that he expired in front of an unfinished canvas.

ideals at the studio of Vien.

This change of mood was evident in Boucher's own lifetime. From as early as 1744, criticisms had been voiced about his cloying sweetness and artificiality. Led by Diderot, his detractors became more outspoken over the years, culminating in the former making a bitter attack on Boucher in 1765.

FAILING EYESIGHT

Boucher was unable to respond effectively to Diderot since, by this time, his powers were beginning to desert him and from the mid-1750s, his eyesight had started to fail. Despite this, official recognition of his achievements continued unabated. In 1755, he succeeded Oudry as Director of the Gobelins tapestry factory and, in the following year, he was called upon by Falconet, the head of the royal porcelain works, to give new impetus to the enterprise, after its relocation at Sèvres.

Even after the death of Madame de Pompadour, Boucher's career did not wane. In 1765, her brother, the Marquis de Marigny, secured for him the post of King's Painter following the death of Carle van Loo and, at the same time, he also acquired the vacant Directorship of the Academy.

In fact, Boucher was both too busy and too infirm to do justice to these honours and he delegated most of his duties to an associate named Cochin. In 1766, he unwisely travelled to Holland, to advise an old friend on the purchase of some paintings. This was only the second occasion on which he had been outside France, but it proved a great strain, weakening his frail constitution still further and probably contributing to his death on 30 May 1770, in his studio at the Louvre.

Carle Van Loo/The Artist at Work/Versailles

A Master of Sensuality

Seen in the context of the frivolous times prior to the French Revolution, Boucher's works provide the ideal accompaniment to the finery of the extravagant ruling classes he served.

Landscape with Figures Gathering Cherries (1768)
(below) With seemingly careless grace, Boucher could turn an innocent subject like this into a painting of luxurious and abandoned sensuality with its overturned pots, grass like silken sheets, and the lascivious gaze of the young man as he drops the cherries into the girl's lap.

The eclipse of Boucher's popularity after the French Revolution was part of the price he had to pay for being an artist of his own time. So closely was he identified with the life of Louis XV and his circle, that a true evaluation of his worth was not possible until the frivolities of the Ancien Régime were sufficiently distant to appear quaint rather than decadent. This rediscovery was brought about by the Goncourt brothers in 1862.

By then, however, many of the original settings for Boucher's works had been swept away and the paintings themselves dispersed into private collections. The original settings were in the new aristocratic mansions that sprung up around Paris after the departure of the Court from Versailles,

when public taste shifted away from the grandiose Baroque style and settled on a more intimate and decorative manner.

Most of Boucher's paintings were intended for specific locations – above panelling or doors – and were designed to blend in with both the architecture and the furniture. This decorative function dictated both the subject and the treatment of his work; a colourful scene of a bathing goddess was always more fitting for a bathroom than a serious piece of moralizing. For this reason, it is easier to gain a fair impression of Boucher's qualities from those few works still remaining in situ – such as Newby Hall, an Adam house in Yorkshire, where tapestries of Boucher's

Landscape with Watermill (1743)
(below) Although criticised for artificiality, Boucher's beautiful landscapes were often based on sketches from the countryside around Beauvais – this picture includes the mill at Charenton. The silvery light and the elements of fantasy (such as the classic temple) were added later in the studio.

The National Trust, Waddesdon Manor

Musée des Beaux-Arts, Lille

Louis Philippe Joseph, duc de Montpensier (c.1750)

(above) The duc de Montpensier, later the duc d'Orleans, grew up to become 'Philippe Egalité', one of the key figures of the French Revolution. He was guillotined in 1793.

Half-naked Woman Bending Over

(above right) Despite Joshua Reynold's assertion to the contrary, Boucher's nudes were based on real models and crayon or chalk sketches like this were collected avidly by both men and women.

Loves of the Gods were ordered direct from the Gobelins tapestry works in the 1760s – rather than from the cold environment of a gallery.

Boucher's decorative style was built up from many different sources. In addition to the early influences of Lemoyne, Watteau and the Italians, he drew much inspiration from Dutch art and, in particular, from Abraham Bloemaert. While in Italy, he purchased a number of drawings by the latter and used them for a series of etchings in 1735. From Bloemaert, Boucher acquired the bustling, animated quality of his work and also, perhaps, the decorous sense of disorder, which the Goncourts termed 'le fouillis'.

A TASTE FOR THE EXOTIC

Boucher's development was also fashioned by his wide-ranging links with the applied arts and, especially, with tapestry and the theatre. His work for the Gobelins factory at Beauvais occupied him intermittently for most of his career and to it he brought his characteristic, lighthearted approach. Breaking with the sombre academic style, he introduced bright pastel shades, notably of pink and blue.

Boucher's main duties for the Gobelins were at the designing stage. Thus, for example, at the 1742 Salon he exhibited eight studies, in oil on canvas, depicting scenes of Chinese life. Ostensibly, these were based on the drawings of the Jesuit traveller, Father Attiret, but, in fact, they owed more to the exotic fantasies of Boucher's imagination. Six of these scenes were accepted as prototypes for tapestries. The result was Boucher's first series of chinoiserie tapestries, which were deemed so successful that Louis XV actually presented a set to

Louvre, Paris

Woman with Muff

(above) Uncharacteristically sombre in colour and plain in composition, this delightful portrait nonetheless shows Boucher's beautiful, silvery light and his masterly rendition of luxurious textures.

The Bowes Museum, Barnard Castle

Diana after Bathing (1742)
(left and detail right) Like so many artists, Boucher dug casually into classical myths simply to find a hook for his own visual style. His Diana, *one of his finest paintings, shows not the mythical huntress, but a nude young woman who has stepped straight from an 18th century salon, scarcely waiting to discard her satins and pearls; the face may even be a portrait. Boucher captures perfectly the contemporary ideal of soft, feminine sensuality and the pale, naked flesh positively glows. Meanwhile, the references to Diana as huntress – the bow and arrows, the dogs and the kill – are strewn around the borders of the picture with all the easy precision of a still life composition.*

Louvre, Paris

the Chinese emperor, Chien Lung.

There was a fair degree of interchange between Boucher's various artistic media. Several of his stage designs were reworked as tapestries and, by the same token, some of his plans for the latter ended up as paintings. X-rays have shown that his large picture, *The Rising of the Sun* (p.96) was initially executed in *grisaille* (monochrome relief), while its companion piece, *The Setting of the Sun* (p.97) was produced normally. The grisaille format indicates that *The Rising* was intended as a tapestry cartoon, but was diverted from this by the purchaser, Madame de Pompadour, who then commissioned the second painting.

CLASSIC FANTASIES

Much less survives of Boucher's work for the theatre although it was of crucial importance. In particular, it accounts for the shallow, set-like construction of most of his compositions. Usually, the action is thrown well to the fore of his paintings, with very little penetration behind. In the case of the mythological works, identifying attributes, such as Diana's arrows or Venus's shells, are prominently displayed at the edges of the pictures, adding to their sense of artificiality.

Given the kind of themes that Boucher had to work with, his air of fantasy was hardly misplaced. *Issé*, for instance – for which some of his scenery designs still exist – was a romantic fable, borrowed from Ovid, which told of Apollo disguising himself as a shepherd in order to seduce his mortal

---

COMPARISONS

Diana the Huntress

Over the centuries, many artists have been drawn to the subject of Diana, the virgin goddess. In Roman myth, Diana (known as Artemis to the Greeks) is associated with the moon, the symbol of her chastity, and with hunting. It is the combination of predatory skill and virgin beauty that normally attracts artists, and most portray her in an active role, involved in the chase or taking revenge on those who spy on her while bathing; Boucher's passive, 'feminine' nude is unusual.

Peter Paul Rubens (1577-1640)
The Nymphs of Diana Surprised by Satyrs
(right) In Rubens' painting, a fierce Diana is depicted on the right, about to hurl her spear at the rapacious satyrs. In contrast to Boucher's tranquil scene, Rubens' frieze-like composition is full of swirling energy and movement, with powerful diagonals sweeping across the picture.

love. A casual approach to the classics permeates Boucher's work.

The fashion for decoration played very much in Boucher's favour. His infrequent attempts at religious or history-painting demonstrate how uncomfortable he felt with such themes. This lack of serious moral purpose was the nub of Diderot's criticisms of Boucher, although his celebrated complaint that the artist had never looked at nature was not strictly accurate.

The abundance of sketches and drawings indicate that, however artificial the end result, Boucher was both diligent and meticulous in his studies of nature. He was the first artist to market his drawings successfully in the Salon, where his red and black drawings of women, in chalk or in crayon, sold prolifically. These beautiful and perceptive studies give the lie to the misconceptions that later arose as a result of the surprised comments of Joshua Reynolds who, on the single occasion when he visited the artist in his studio, found him working without a model.

Boucher's true attitude to nature can be seen most clearly from his sensitive landscape drawings, most of which were sketched in the Picardy countryside around Beauvais or on his trips to Charenton with Oudry. It was only afterwards, in the studio, that he added classical motifs to transform them from simple nature studies into his own heady dreamworld.

Fontainebleau School (c.1550) Diana the Huntress

(right) This panel painting is one of the finest works of the artists brought together by Francis I at Fontainebleau in the 16th century, and is typical of their interest in heroic mythology. The Fontainebleau Diana is vigorous and athletic, almost manly, and her cool, asexual gaze is completely unlike the misty-eyed sensuality of Boucher's young goddess.

Prado, Madrid

Louvre, Paris

Decoration

The decorative motifs that appear throughout Boucher's work were culled from his vast collection of *objets trouvé*.

THE MAKING OF A MASTERPIECE

Mademoiselle O'Murphy

This beautiful, unaffected nude, sometimes known simply as *Reclining Girl*, shows Boucher at the height of his powers in 1752. The ideal of soft, feminine sensuality that pervades all Boucher's pictures here hangs in the air like heady perfume, and the opalescent flesh of the young girl is almost tangible. It is one of many pictures he painted of reclining nudes; indeed several versions of this particular work exist. And the completely uninhibited pose of the girl belies the care that has gone into the composition, with gentle diagonals running lazily across the picture to enhance the dream-like quality.

Joachim Blauel-Artothek

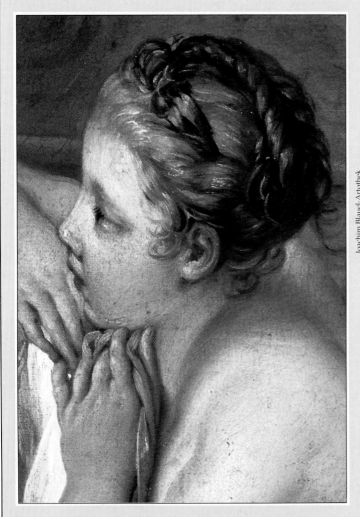

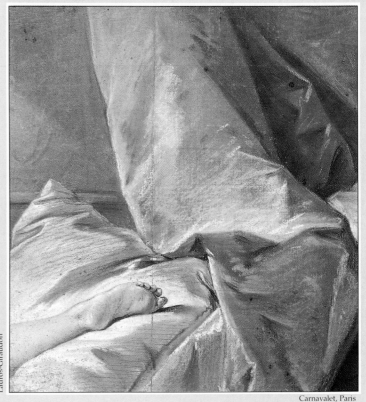

Cherubic face
(above) The model for this painting is usually identified as 14-year-old Louise O'Murphy, the daughter of an Irish cobbler. Despite the cherubic face, she modelled for Boucher, was mistress to Louis XV, and is mentioned in Casanova's memoirs.

A well-drawn foot
(right) Behind the sketchy, almost casual rendering of details, such as the girl's foot, lies a lifetime of careful study of female anatomy in accurate preparatory sketches. Altogether, Boucher made over 10,000 drawings of various subjects.

Lauros-Giraudon

Carnavalet, Paris

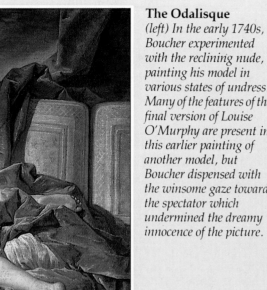

Réunion des Musées Nationaux

The Odalisque
(left) In the early 1740s, Boucher experimented with the reclining nude, painting his model in various states of undress. Many of the features of the final version of Louise O'Murphy are present in this earlier painting of another model, but Boucher dispensed with the winsome gaze towards the spectator which undermined the dreamy innocence of the picture.

Louvre, Paris

> 'Voluptuousness is the essence of Boucher's ideal.'
>
> Edmond and Jules de Goncourt

Alte Pinakothek, Munich

Early sketch
(above) As this preparatory sketch shows, Boucher could draw from life brilliantly. In the final painting, Boucher made Louise subtly chubbier – note the hands – to emphasize both her youth and the softness and delicacy of her naked flesh.

Rumpled drapery
(right) Casually draped silks and satins are one of the hallmarks of Boucher's work and he uses them again and again to suggest the pampered lassitude of his naked women, capturing their luxurious texture with just a few deft brushstrokes.

Gallery

Like Rubens before him and Renoir after, Boucher placed his art at the service of pleasure. He delighted in beautiful women, usually nude, voluptuous and flushed with health and vitality. Works such as The Triumph of Venus, The Rising of the Sun, and The Setting of the Sun are visions of the happiest of all possible worlds that he and his patrons, the court and aristocracy that was to be swept away in the French Revolution, could imagine. They certainly tell us more about the fantasy life of the 'old régime' than about their actual subject-matter, for Boucher used his sources in classical mythology with a quite unscholarly freedom. The goddess of love is the absolute monarch of his world, and it is the earthly version of love rather than the spiritual that she embodies, as spread abroad by her dimpled, throughly naughty son, Cupid. Everyone is her subject, from the nymphs and putti who wait upon her, to the ever-amorous shepherds and shepherdesses who inhabit Boucher's countryside, to the contemporary women in their flirtatious finery whom we see in genre scenes such as Le Déjeuner and La Modiste.

The Triumph of Venus *1740*
64″ × 51″ Nationalmuseum, Stockholm

Enthroned upon a chariot borne through the waves by tritons and dolphins, Venus' 'triumph' recalls her birth – she was born out of the sea and drifted ashore on a scallop shell. She and her attendant sea-nymphs inhabit an impossible floating world where the sea becomes a blue-green velvet couch on which to recline seductively, and the sky is alive with putti, the mischievous angels of earthly love. One of the nymphs offers up pearls in tribute to her mistress but Venus is distracted by her son, Cupid, who is up to his usual tricks and making another nymph fall in love, firing his victim's affections for some unseen male with just a touch, as if playing a game of tag. Venus' wistful, pitying expression may mean that she foresees painful consequences. Her features are said to be those of the artist's wife.

Le Déjeuner *1739*
32¼″ × 25½″ Louvre, Paris

Madame Boucher takes morning chocolate, with her two children, a maid and a young servant. The interior decoration is typically rococo and beside the mirror are cabinets containing part of the artist's collection of exotic objects, including a Buddha. The fall of light from the window, in particular, recalls Dutch painting.

La Modiste *1746*
25″ × 21″ Nationalmuseum, Stockholm

*This is the only surviving work from a set of four representing the
Times of Day in scenes from everyday life. It is morning and a lady,
having just finished dressing her hair, examines the latest fashionable
knick-knacks brought by a milliner. The set was commissioned from
Boucher by Count Tessin, the Swedish ambassador in Paris.*

Mademoiselle O'Murphy 1752
23″ × 28¾″ Alte Pinakothek, Munich

'White like a lily,' wrote Casanova of Mademoiselle O'Murphy, 'she possessed all the beauty that nature or the painter's art could possibly bestow.' She was of Irish origin, worked as an artist's model in Paris from an early age, posing for Boucher probably when she was fourteen, and later became the mistress of Louis XV. As a frankly erotic portrait-nude, making no pretence to illustrate some classical myth or allegory, Boucher's painting is an obvious forerunner of the modern pin-up photograph. The design is full of curves, and the forms of the girl's body find echoes in those of the couch and the panelling behind her. The Chinese incense-burner heightens the air of sensuality by adding delightful aromas for us to imagine, and the little dragon on the lid turns up towards Mademoiselle O'Murphy as if transfixed by her beauty.

93

The Bridge 1751
26″ × 33¼″ Louvre, Paris

From a limited range of favourite elements, dilapidated bridges and watermills, the occasional dovecote, and plenty of rustic woodwork, Boucher creates a charmingly ramshackle vision of Arcadia.

The Mill 1751
26″ × 33¼″ Louvre, Paris

Boucher's is the same comic-opera conception of country life that inspired Marie Antoinette to have a picturesque farm built in the gardens of Versailles and wear a fanciful milkmaid's outfit.

The Rising of the Sun *1753*
126½" × 106½" Wallace Collection, London

*This composition was originally painted in monochrome. Boucher
seems to have overpainted it in colour, then executed its companion-
piece in colour from the start, on commission from Madame de
Pompadour. The pair are his grandest works. His beloved sea-nymphs
prepare Apollo for his daily journey across the sky.*

The Setting of the Sun 1753
127½″ × 104″ Wallace Collection, London

*Apollo returns and steps from his Rococo chariot into
the arms of a sea-nymph, probably Thetis, in a setting
more reminiscent of a boudoir than the surface of the
ocean. If the day is for duty, Boucher seems to say,
then the night is for pleasure.*

Madame de Pompadour *1758*
84″ × 65″ Alte Pinakothek, Munich

*Boucher's portraits of Madame de Pompadour celebrate a mature and
dignified kind of beauty, quite different from that of his Venuses and
nymphs. She is allowed a mind, and shown in a setting that suggests
conversation and the arts rather than sex. We are thus reminded that
we are in the presence of a woman of culture.*

Madame de Pompadour *1759*
36″ × 27″ Wallace Collection, London

The Marquise is shown in the gardens of her home, the Château de Bellevue. The marble group in the background was commissioned by her from the sculptor Pigalle and represents Love and Friendship. A matronly 'Friendship' rebuffs the hot advances of Cupid, symbolizing the way her relationship with Louis XV had matured.

Madame de Pompadour

A figure of immense power at the court of Louis XV, Madame de Pompadour matched her astute political acumen with an intelligent and invaluable contribution to the arts in 18th-century France.

Jeanne-Antoinette Poisson, better known as Madame de Pompadour, was born in Paris in 1721. Her father was a speculator who fled the country following a black-market scandal, leaving his daughter in the care of Le Normant de Tournehem. This wealthy financier saw his ward's future in royal circles and proceeded to gear her education towards becoming a king's mistress. Jeanne-Antoinette married her guardian's nephew which brought her the title Madame d'Etioles and gave her an introduction at court. Soon after, at a masked ball at Versailles to celebrate the marriage of the Dauphin, she met the King and, from that moment on, de Tournehem's prophecies were to become a reality. The tall, slim, blonde Madame

Jean Loup Charmet

George de la Tour/Edimedia

Maurice Quentin de Latour; Louvre/Réunion des Musées Nationaux

Madame's private theatre
(above) Madame de Pompadour often entertained the King and favoured courtiers in the little blue and silver theatre in her own apartment. Here she is singing in Acis and Galatéa *with the Vicomte de Rohan, while the King and his friends follow the opera in the libretto.*

A regal couple
(left and above left) When 23-year-old Jeanne-Antoinette Poisson captivated Louis XV, she more than fulfilled the prophecy of her guardian that she would become a king's mistress. Her energy, education and natural gifts ensured her position at court for 20 years – and her name as legend forever after.

d'Etioles found herself with Louis, who, for a number of reasons, was more than ready to begin a new liaison.

The Queen had given birth to an heir to the throne and had made it quite clear that she no longer intended to sleep with the King. And Louis' young mistress, the Duchesse de Chateauroux, had recently died in tragic circumstances, so Madame d'Etioles obtained a legal separation from her husband and moved into a small apartment in Versailles, connected to the King's chambers by a discreet staircase.

The King enjoyed the intimacy of these modest surroundings but it certainly caused problems. Government ministers might find themselves pursuing him up the staircase, often to be ejected on the grounds that the King was 'tired'. Further,

Musée Voltaire, Genève/Edimage

the intimate suppers held for the King in Madame d'Etioles' apartment could only accommodate a select few. And the small makeshift theatre she instigated, which staged many notable premieres including that of Moliere's *Tartuffe*, seated only 20. This meant that most of the French aristocracy, which numbered around 400, were excluded.

THE KING'S CHOICE

Though Louis had made it his business to seduce chambermaids, until this time he had restricted his choice of *maîtresse declarée* to the ladies of the court. Only they knew how to walk properly, curtsy in the approved manner and talk with the distinct accent and vocabulary of *ce pays-ci* (this country), as the court was called. Few thought that the King's attention could be held by one so obviously out of place. But soon those excluded from the King's inner circle by this 'little bourgeoise' grew resentful and commissioned songs and pamphlets ridiculing her – her maiden name of Poisson, meaning fish, was a gift. But Jeanne-Antoinette's vivacious conversation, her singing and acting ability, and her love of the arts captivated the King. Formerly, the only recreation he had enjoyed – apart from the joys of seduction – was foxhunting. She introduced him to the pleasures of gardening, the appreciation of art, the manufacture of Sèvres porcelain, literature and

Bulloz

Literary patronage
(above) The French writer Voltaire was indebted to Madame de Pompadour for her unfailing loyalty in promoting his interests, and for her understanding of him. She perceived the gifts that were masked by a somewhat difficult personality, and he ultimately repaid her by the description that could almost be her epitaph: 'Sincère et tendre Pompadour'.

The Sèvres factory
(left) Madame de Pompadour loved china as much as she loved flowers – and she filled her rooms with both. Her founding of the Sèvres factory was her most lasting achievement, and certainly the most profitable for France.

architecture with some measure of success. Both Boucher and Voltaire were introduced to court at her instigation. And in May 1747, the King created her Marquise de Pompadour. Just 23, the 'little bourgeoise' had become an aristocrat.

As much as she loved the King, Madame de Pompadour soon found herself exhausted by Louis' ardour. At first she tried eating aphrodisiacs like truffles, crayfish and vanilla. But instead of becoming passionate, she simply made herself sick. And her flagging sexual appetite made her extremely vulnerable. Enemies in court – like the Comte d'Argenson and Madame d'Estrades – plotted against her by bringing in young mistresses, like the ravishing 18-year-old Comtesse de Choiseul-Romanet, to seduce the King. But after using her political wiles to see off these threats, Madame de Pompadour solved the problem in the long term by bringing in a succession of her own young, pretty – but empty-headed – women to satisfy Louis' excessive demands. She managed to retain his attention through her good company and her level-headed advice. Soon she became his trusted confidante and adviser.

Versailles/Réunion des Musées Nationaux

ROYAL RECOGNITION

This situation became regularized in October 1755 when, following the death of her daughter by her former marriage and her return to the Catholic church, she stopped being Louis' mistress. One of the few people in the court who knew about this eventuality was the Queen who consented to allowing Madame de Pompadour to take the post of lady-in-waiting. The King also made her a duchess.

Madame de Pompadour's problems were not yet over, however. She was unpopular with the French people who held her responsible for many of the political catastrophes of the era. So when, early in 1757, an assassin called Damien stabbed

the King, it had, of course, to be Madame de Pompadour's fault. Believing he was dying, Louis confessed his sins and renounced his former infidelity. Without the King's full support Madame de Pompadour found her position at court was no longer tenable and prepared to leave Versailles. But a mob rushed towards the palace shouting: 'Long live the King' and 'Death to Madame de Pompadour'. Friends persuaded her not to leave – and when the King recovered, there was a reconciliation.

In fact, it was her political influence that was eventually to break her spirit. A frank and faithful adviser in a court full of intrigue, the King naturally depended on her impartial opinions. Although Louis made most of the decisions, they were often

The Palace of Versailles
(above) Louis XV's splendid palace was also Madame de Pompadour's first residence as mistress-in-chief. The view from her balcony would have been very much the same as it is today, but her rooms – on the second floor of the north wing – were then full of life and entertainment, a mirror of her varied political and artistic interests.

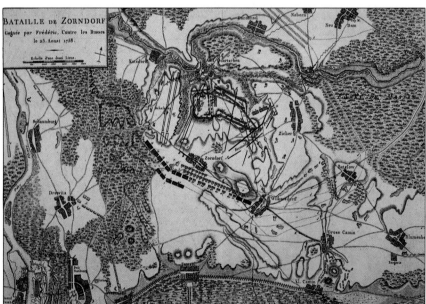

Giancarlo Costa

The Battle of Zorndorf
(left) One of the battles of the Seven Years' War particularly involved the Russians, who fought with great spirit but at great cost. Half the army fell while a third of the Prussians were either killed or wounded.

The Battle of Hochkirch
(right) Two months later the Austrians surrounded the Prussian camp. A desperate struggle ensued, from which the Austrian army emerged too shaken to press their advantage.

Archiv für Kunst und Geschichte

executed by Madame de Pompadour and her favourites were moved into positions of power. And this gave the impression that she was running the country. So when one of her protégés, Duc de Choiseul, instigated the 'Reversal of Alliances' allying France with its old enemy Austria against the protestant German states, which led to the Seven Years' war, the disastrous consequences of the war were blamed on Madame de Pompadour.

'APRÈS NOUS LE DÉLUGE'

No longer able to put on a brave face, she retired to her apartments. Her comment to Louis on the situation was '*Après nous le deluge*' (After us the deluge). And so it was to be. The glory she had so desperately wanted for the King and for France had ended in shame and ruination. 'If I die', she is recorded as saying, 'it will be of grief.'

Soon after the end of the war she did die. Not from grief, but probably from lung cancer. During her last days her old enemy the Dauphin wrote 'She is dying with a courage rare for either sex. Her lungs are full of water, or pus and the heart congested or dilated, it is an unbelievably cruel and painful death.'

Though the King was not with her during her last hours, he did give his permission for her to die in Versailles, a privilege usually restricted to members of the royal family. And when the day of her funeral arrived and the cortège was ready to leave for Paris, where she was to be buried, he watched from his balcony. A storm raged and he is said to have remarked: 'The Marquise has bad weather for her journey.' Tears were seen pouring down the King's face – a final tribute to his departed mistress of nearly 20 years.

Afterwards Voltaire wrote of Madame de Pompadour: 'Born sincere, she loved the King for himself; she had righteousness in her soul and justice in her heart; all this is not to be met with every day . . . It is the end of a dream.'

A fatal alliance
(right) An image, engraved by Madame de Pompadour's own hand, of the Austrian-French alliance which brought about her downfall. She was made the scapegoat for the shameful and bloody struggle in which France and other European states became involved against Frederick of Prussia.

A later portrait
(below) François Hubert Drouais' portrait does full justice to the grace, charm and creative interests which remained with Madame de Pompadour right into middle age.

Fotomas

Attributed to Drouais; Chantilly/Bulloz

In 1758, Boucher's patron, Madame de Pompadour, at the height of her influence in matters cultural, was also taking an interest in the conduct of the Seven Years' War. Unfortunately, France's lack of any firm strategy in the face of British aggression overseas led to disastrous colonial losses during this year.

Valiant Virginian
(below) George Washington was only 21 when he first became involved fighting the French encroachment into Ohio Valley lands claimed by the English Crown. These included the fort of the Ohio Company, renamed Fort Duquesne. The courageous young officer was noticed by successive British generals and rose to the rank of colonel in command of all Virginia troops in spring 1758. In this capacity he acted with General John Forbes to finally oust the French from Fort Duquesne.

New Foreign Minister
(right) A favourite of Madame de Pompadour, the newly created Duc de Choiseul was entrusted with the conduct of the Seven Years War instead of the pessimistic de Bernis. Choiseul found himself faced with a nearly bankrupt France, an insubstantial navy and an army that had been badly treated and demoralised by a succession of incompetent generals. Although he was to prove himself an able and intelligent administrator, France required a miracle to restore her increasing colonial losses.

Madame la Marquise de Pompadour, Louis XV's erstwhile mistress, had been taking an interest in diplomacy for several years and played a part in negotiating the Franco-Austrian alliance that had been instrumental in sparking off the Seven Years War in 1756. Her charming red lacquer boudoir at Versailles had become a war operations centre where she and the King decided policy, with increasingly alarming effects. On 23 June, despite her encouragement, the Comte de Clermont, in command of the French forces in Europe, was driven back across the Rhine after a heavy defeat at Crefeld by Ferdinand of Brunswick's army of Hanover.

Although he was now safe from French attack, Frederick the Great of Prussia was still conducting a war on two fronts against France's Austrian and Russian allies. Thanks to Prussian

military discipline, he had survived the first two years of war without many setbacks but by 1758 the strain had begun to tell. In the spring Frederick besieged the Moravian stronghold of Olmütz, but was forced to raise the siege and fight off a Russian invasion of his own territories. He succeeded (the Battle of Zorndorf was a bloody draw) but suffered serious losses of a sort that Prussia, unlike the large empires opposing her, could ill afford. Then, in October, he camped in a carelessly chosen position, confident that the normally ultra-cautious Austrians would not risk a night attack. They did, and achieved complete surprise. At the ensuing battle of Hochkirch Frederick was hard put to it to save his army and disengage, losing a quarter of his men and over 100 guns. As both sides settled into winter quarters the outlook for Prussia seemed appropriately bleak.

The war in Europe was only one aspect of a world-wide struggle in which the main protagonists were France and Britain. France backed the Austrians while Britain subsidized Ferdinand of Brunswick and Frederick the Great. While France was deeply involved in Continental operations, by contrast the British Prime Minister, William Pitt the Elder, understood the strategic importance of extending the war onto the colonial front so as to ease pressure on Prussia and Hanover. More importantly, Prussian belligerence in Europe made it an easier task for Britain to make colonial conquests at France's expense.

Pitt was brilliant at co-ordinating large-scale operations, and by 1758 his planning had begun to produce spectacular results. Hit-and-run raids on St Malo and Cherbourg destroyed quantities of shipping and tied down many French troops.

Versailles

Réunion des Musées Nationaux

Pombal's vengeance
(below) During 1750-7 Portugal was effectively ruled by the Marquis de Pombal who was determined to eradicate opposition from the nobility and the Jesuits. An attempt on the life of José I on 3 September 1758 gave him his opportunity. The Marquis of Tavora, other nobles and 13 Jesuit priests, including the fiery Malagrida, were all arrested for complicity, three of the nobility and their servants being publicly executed. Pombal then expelled the Jesuit order from Portugal and in 1761 condemned Malagrida to be burnt at the stake as a heretic.

Archives de France

Jean-Loup Charmet

The struggle for Madras
(above) The French finally sent an army out to India early in 1758 under the Comte de Lally. He soon took Fort St David but then foolishly delayed an attack on Madras until October – the beginning of the monsoon season. Governor Pigot and Commander Lawrence had profited by the delay and successfully defended the town until a British squadron appeared offshore the following March, forcing Lally to retire.

Louisbourg recaptured
(right) The fortress of Louisbourg, captured and returned to the French during the War of the Austrian Succession, was again under seige in 1758. Brigadier Wolfe and Admiral Boscawen launched a joint attack on the fortress which guarded the Atlantic approach to New France. It surrendered after seven weeks, thus leaving the way open for Wolfe to capture Quebec in 1759.

Bibliothèque Nationale

Jean-Loup Charmet

Bibliothèque Nationale

Jean-Loup Charmet

Moreover, the British navy succeeded in bottling up the French fleets at Toulon and Brest, thus isolating French colonies outside Europe.

THE STRUGGLE FOR NEW FRANCE

The largest and most active theatre of operations was North America, where the French were grimly holding a long line of forts along the Great Lakes and the Ohio River. Here, too, Pitt made plans on a grand scale, hoping to capture Quebec and Montreal before the year was out. The key to Quebec was the fortress of Louisbourg on Cape Breton Island, which controlled the mouth of the St Lawrence River. The British arrived with 13,000 men and a fleet of 36 ships, but Louisbourg's military and natural defences were so formidable that the attackers needed a good deal of luck if they were even to get ashore. However, the landing was made, led by Brigadier James Wolfe, the beachhead secured and the French driven back. Louisbourg managed to hold out for seven long weeks before finally capitulating on 27 July.

Some 700 miles south, one of Pitt's plans was going wrong. Ineptly led by General Abercrombie, a mixed force of British regulars and colonials failed to take Fort Ticonderoga on Lake Champlain. This setback was partly redeemed by another mixed force under General John Forbes which marched west from Philadelphia to reach Fort Duquesne in November. The French promptly abandoned the fort and Forbes renamed it Pittsburgh in honour of the British Prime Minister.

Giancarlo Costa

National Maritime Museum, Greenwich

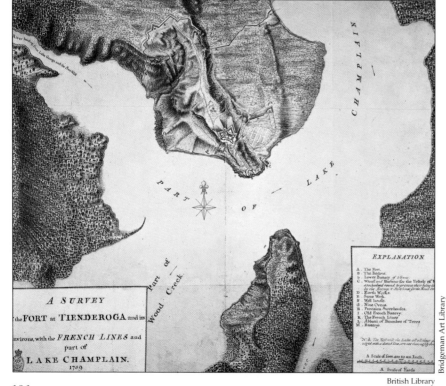

A SURVEY the FORT at TIENDEROGA and its environs, with the FRENCH LINES and part of LAKE CHAMPLAIN. 1759.

Bridgeman Art Library

British Library

British attack on Senegal

(above) By the end of the 17th century, Britain and France were struggling for control of the lucrative slave trade to the Americas, originally set up by the Dutch West India Company. Both had established trading colonies and forts along the Gold coast and it was inevitable that the area would become another source of conflict between the two great powers. In May 1758 a small British force under Commander Keppel took Senegal itself and three weeks later successfully attacked the French strategic naval base on the island of Gorée, just off Cape Verde in Senegal.

Montcalm's greatest victory

(left) In 1758 British troops under the command of General Abercrombie were instructed to take the French fort of Ticonderoga, established two years before on Lake Champlain. The British assault, however, was a disaster. About 500 men of the Black Watch were killed or wounded on becoming enmeshed in a log barricade of felled trees with which the French commander, Montcalm, had surrounded the fort, manned as it was by only 3,800 men. About 2000 British casualties were recorded and honour was only salvaged by the successful capture of Ticonderoga the next year.

Fragonard.

1732-1806

Jean-Honoré Fragonard was the last great painter of the French Rococo style. After a four-year apprenticeship with François Boucher, the favourite painter of Madame de Pompadour, Fragonard won the coveted Prix de Rome, and in 1756 he went to Rome to study. There, he found his greatest source of inspiration in the exuberant works by the Italian Baroque painters, developing a particular admiration for Tiepolo and Pietro da Cortona.

On his return to Paris Fragonard gained membership of the Academy with a large history painting, which also won acclaim at the Salon. He did not, however, follow up this success, but turned to painting on a more intimate scale, specializing in lively erotic pictures which won him a secure market among the Parisian bourgeoisie. But with the onset of the Revolution, Fragonard fell from favour.

'The Amiable Frago'

A light-hearted, charming and witty man, Fragonard was universally popular. His exuberant character is reflected in his paintings, which vividly evoke the gaieties of 18th-century France.

Jean-Honoré Fragonard was born on 5 April 1732 in the village of Grasse, in the Provence region of France. The colourful Provençal landscape with its lush vegetation and dazzling light made a lasting impression on Fragonard, fostering his love of bright colour and inspiring the luxuriant settings of many of his works. The idyllic Mediterranean climate probably also helped to cultivate the easygoing temperament which endeared him to his friends and patrons.

When Fragonard was still a young boy his father, François, a glove-maker by trade, lost his entire income in an ill-fated scheme to promote the use of fire engines. In 1738 the family moved to Paris in an attempt to recover their fortunes, and François took a job as a haberdasher's assistant. When Fragonard was 15, he was sent to work as a junior clerk in the office of a Paris lawyer. He was not, however, suited to such routine work and spent his time drawing caricatures until his employer persuaded the boy's parents to allow him to pursue an artistic education.

Fragonard's mother took him to the studio of François Boucher, a fashionable painter of erotic and pastoral scenes. But Boucher was unwilling to accept an untrained pupil, so Fragonard began his apprenticeship with Jean-Baptiste Chardin, a brilliant artist who specialized in finely executed genre scenes. Chardin encouraged his pupils to learn by copying from contemporary prints, and coached them in his own meticulous technique. Fragonard soon became unhappy with this rigorous discipline and after six months he left

Jean-Loup Charmet

A debt to Provence
(below) Fragonard was born in Grasse, the centre of the perfume industry. The vivid colours of the Provençal landscape and the warmth and gaiety of the region reappear in Fragonard's paintings.

Changing fortunes
(above) When Fragonard was six, the family was forced to move to Paris, where his father tried unsuccessfully to recover some of the money he had lost in a speculative enterprise.

Key Dates

1732 born in Grasse, Provence

1738 moves to Paris

1747 begins apprenticeship with Chardin

1748 enters Boucher's studio

1752 wins the Prix de Rome

1756-60 studies in Rome

1760 spends the summer at Tivoli with Saint-Non; travels to Venice and Naples

1761 returns to Paris

1765 becomes member of the Academy

1766/67 paints *The Swing*

1769 marries Marie-Anne Gérard

1773 second trip to Italy

1775 Marguerite Gérard joins the household

1789 outbreak of the French Revolution

1792 son enters David's studio

1793 elected to the Museums Commission

1806 dies in Paris

H. Daries/Top

Wallace Collection, London

Fragonard's teachers
(right and left) In 1747 Fragonard began his training with Chardin (right), but his impetuous temperament was unsuited to Chardin's laborious teaching methods, and he soon left. The following year he was accepted by Boucher, whose pastoral scenes such as Shepherd Piping to a Shepherdess *(left) strongly influenced him.*

Baroque inspiration
(below) After winning the Prix de Rome, Fragonard spent four years studying the Italian Masters. He was particularly impressed by the turbulent works of Baroque painters such as Pietro da Cortona.

Chardin: Self-Portrait/Louvre, Paris

Chardin's studio and continued his education alone, copying paintings in churches and private collections around Paris. Finally, in 1748, Boucher agreed to take him on.

Boucher was then at the height of his popularity. He was the favourite painter of Madame de Pompadour, Louis XV's mistress, and was in enormous demand for his richly decorative panels. He seems to have given Fragonard little formal tuition but set him to work on the large-scale designs for tapestries produced by his workshop for the famous Gobelins factory. Boucher was clearly impressed by Fragonard's talent and in 1752, despite Fragonard's lack of academic training, he advised him to enter for the coveted Prix de Rome. With characteristic virtuosity, Fragonard produced a masterly religious canvas in the required 'grand style', and was awarded the prize, which included a trip to Rome, at his first attempt.

AN ITALIAN TRAINING

Before going to the Ecole de Rome, Fragonard spent a statutory four years at the Ecole des Elèves Protégés, an academic school designed to prepare young prize-winners for their confrontation with the revered Italian Old Masters. In December 1756 he arrived in Rome with his fellow students, who included Boucher's pupil and son-in-law, Jean-Baptiste Deshayes.

Fragonard's first few years in Rome were unsettled and unproductive. He confessed himself overwhelmed and discouraged by the works of Raphael and Michelangelo and was ill-at-ease with the long-established practice of drawing from casts and copying classical statues. He was more at home with the freedom and exuberance of the

Pietro da Cortona: Frescoed ceiling/Barberini Palace, Rome

great Baroque painters and made several copies after the works of the 17th-century painter, Pietro da Cortona.

The director of the school, Charles-Joseph Natoire, was an enlightened and sympathetic man who, despite his anxieties about Fragonard's progress, allowed him to go his own way. But it was not until 1760, under the generous patronage of the Abbé de Saint-Non, that Fragonard truly realized his own gifts. The Abbé was a wealthy and affable character, and an accomplished amateur artist who had come to Rome to broaden his experience of Italian culture. On meeting Fragonard, probably through Natoire, he seems to have recognized the artist's brilliant if unruly talent and invited Fragonard to travel to Venice with him at his own expense. Before setting out, they spent the summer at the magnificent Villa d'Este at Tivoli, together with Hubert Robert, a gifted landscape painter who became one of Fragonard's closest friends. From Tivoli, the three men travelled to Venice. Fragonard then travelled alone to Naples, copying the great Baroque masters, with ever-increasing confidence, in pen-and-ink sketches which were later published at Saint-Non's own expense.

In the autumn of 1761, Fragonard and Saint-Non returned to Paris. For the next few years Fragonard worked in relative obscurity, painting genre and pastoral scenes and building his sketches of Tivoli into large compositions, such as *The Gardens of the Villa d'Este* (p.120). In 1765 however, he scored his first public success with a

The Abbé de Saint-Non

Fragonard's meeting with the Abbé de Saint-Non proved to be a turning-point in his career. The Abbé was a discerning collector and a keen amateur artist, and his generous and undemanding patronage gave the artist his first opportunity of working outside an academic environment. At Saint-Non's expense Fragonard was left to work as he pleased, first at the magnificent Villa d'Este and later in his travels to Venice and Naples. The Abbé also financed the publication of some of Fragonard's sketches, and purchased several of his paintings.

Inspiration
(left) Fragonard's superb portrait of Saint-Non also represents the art of Poetry – a fitting tribute to the artist's cultured patron.

The Villa d'Este
(right) In 1760 Fragonard and Saint-Non spent the summer drawing at the splendid Villa d'Este at Tivoli. The villa's rambling landscape garden provided the perfect material for Fragonard's spontaneous, 'sketchy' style (p.120).

Louvre, Paris

Reunion des Musees-Nationaux

Academic acclaim
(left) This melodramatic painting of Coresus Sacrificing Himself to Save Callirhoe *was painted for the Governor of the King's Buildings and exhibited at the Salon in 1765. It was enthusiastically received by the critics and ensured Fragonard a place at the Academy. The subject is the heroic action of Coresus, the high priest of Bacchus, who has stepped in to save his beloved Callirhoe from being sacrificed in an attempt to ward off the plague.*

Louvre, Paris

The Visit to the Nursery/Samuel H. Kress Collection, National Gallery of Art, Washington

large, melodramatic history painting entitled *Coresus Sacrificing Himself to Save Callirhoe* (opposite). The painting secured Fragonard's membership of the Academy, and was enthusiastically received at the Paris Salon, particularly by the influential critic Diderot who was one of Boucher's fiercest opponents. However, Fragonard did not follow up his success. Although the Governor of the King's Buildings ordered a tapestry reproduction of the painting, payments were slow and Fragonard turned to a more lucrative type of painting.

EROTIC CANVASES

By this time Fragonard seems to have already established a reputation as a painter of erotic scenes, for in 1766 he was commissioned to paint an erotic canvas, now known as *The Swing* (p.121) for the Baron de Saint-Julien. From this point onwards he received a steady stream of commissions for erotic or sensual themes to adorn the salons and boudoirs of actresses, financiers and wealthy connoisseurs.

Fragonard's decision to abandon history painting was not purely a financial one. He was gifted with remarkable technical virtuosity and was at his best when working quickly and allowing his imagination free rein. The undemanding patronage of the wealthy middle class gave him

greater artistic freedom than the rigorous, pedantic world of the Salon. Most important of all, it allowed him to pursue the light-hearted subject-matter with which he was most at home. Fragonard was not an intellectual. He was a practical, energetic man, with a natural charm and a delightful wit. Known to his friends as 'the amiable Frago', he was universally loved and described by a contemporary as 'plump, dapper, always bright and cheerful, with fine rosy cheeks, sparkling eyes and a tousled mat of grey hair'. He added to his personal charms a robust sense of humour and a down-to-earth approach to his art. An acquaintance said of him: 'A painter in every fibre of his being, he felt himself so powerfully driven by the demon of his art that he could say, in words which should be left as they are, because they are his own: "If necessary, I would even paint with my bottom".'

Family scenes
(above) Fragonard married in 1769. His contented home-life, which was shared with his wife's beautiful sister Marguerite, prompted many paintings of happy family scenes which reflect the artist's enjoyment of his own children.

Sophie Guimard/Louvre, Paris

Portrait of a dancer
(left) Sophie Guimard was a famous ballet dancer whose notorious salons were attended by the fashionable élite. She commissioned several works by Fragonard in the early 1770s, including a decorative cycle for the drawing room of her house on the Chaussée d'Antin. But in 1773 the dancer and the artist quarrelled, and Fragonard left the cycle unfinished after taking his revenge by replacing Sophie's smiling features in one of the panels with a portrait of one of the Furies.

Francois-André Vincent: Bergeret de Grancourt/Musée des Beaux-Arts, Besançon

Lauros-Giraudon

Jean-Loup Charmet

During the early 1770s Fragonard produced some of his greatest masterpieces. In 1771 he received a commission from Madame du Barry, who had replaced Madame de Pompadour as Louis XV's mistress, for four panels to decorate the interior of a new garden pavilion at her château at Louveciennes. The magnificent *Pursuit of Love* series (pp.124-5) was returned unexpectedly in 1773 and replaced with a set of insipid panels in the new semi-classical style. Fragonard was gravely disappointed. He took back the panels, refused the payment that was offered and refused to speak of the matter ever again.

Late in 1773, Fragonard went on a second trip to Italy, at the expense of Bergeret de Grancourt, a wealthy financier who was to become an important patron. On his return, Fragonard built his renewed experience of the Italian landscape into a series of superb imaginative compositions such as *The Swing* (p.129) and *Blind Man's Buff* (p.128), both owned by the Abbé de Saint-Non. During this period, possibly under the influence of Marguerite Gérard, he also painted a number of gentle domestic scenes, together with some of his most sensitive and alluring portraits of women, such as the *Woman Reading a Book* (p.127).

By 1780, Fragonard's greatest period of creativity was over. During the previous decade,

In 1767 Fragonard exhibited at the Salon for the second and last time, showing a few drawings, a portrait head and a small canvas of a group of putti. The critics were bitterly disappointed. Diderot described the putti contemptuously as a 'well-cooked omelette' and the following year remarked acidly that Boucher's pupils 'hardly know how to handle a brush or hold a palette before they take to weaving garlands of children, painting chubby pink bottoms and indulging in all sorts of extravagances'. Undeterred, Fragonard continued to paint his erotic masterpieces, such as *The Longed-For Moment* (p.114), together with a series of 'fancy portraits' – portraits of his friends and patrons in exotic costume, painted with astonishing virtuosity and speed (p.116).

DOMESTIC HAPPINESS

In 1769 Fragonard married. His wife, Marie-Anne Gérard, was the elder daughter of a perfumer from Grasse, who had come to Fragonard for instruction in painting. The marriage was a relatively happy one, although Marie-Anne was an unprepossessing woman, and Fragonard later showed a marked preference for her beautiful younger sister, Marguerite. A contemporary described Mme Fragonard as 'a very tall, very stout and very plebeian woman who ruined the few charms that had survived her youth by the most jarring extravagances of the toilet.' Marguerite came to live with the Fragonards in 1775, also to take painting lessons. She was as charming as her sister was ugly, and was much loved by everyone, 'especially by little papa Fragonard'.

An ungracious patron
(above left) Bergeret de Grancourt fell out with Fragonard after their journey to Italy. His demand to keep the artist's sketches in lieu of expenses ended in an unsavoury court case.

Royal connections
(below) In the 1770s Fragonard undertook several decorative commissions for King Louis XV and his mistress, Madame du Barry, at the Court of Versailles.

Revolutionary changes
(above) The outbreak of the Revolution in 1789 brought a new fashion for stoical, revolutionary themes. Fragonard lost many of his aristocratic patrons and his frivolous style became obsolete.

Alain Chisnet/Image Bank

the demand for erotic paintings had gradually declined. Fragonard's exuberant decorative style had also begun to go out of fashion under the influence of the Neo-Classical style, which gained popularity in the years leading up to the French Revolution. When the Revolution broke out in 1789, it did not affect Fragonard dramatically, although he and his family fled to Grasse during the Reign of Terror. They finally returned to Paris in March 1791, and the following year Fragonard's son, Alexandre-Evariste, entered the studio of Jacques-Louis David, the greatest exponent of the Neo-Classical style, and the most influential painter in France.

Despite the radical differences in their artistic outlooks, David and Fragonard were on friendly terms and in 1793 David recommended the elderly artist for an administrative post in the newly formed Museums Commission which had been set up for the purpose of establishing the National Collections. The income from this post, together with the money from a few portraits and family scenes, allowed Fragonard to live in relative comfort, and he was given free accommodation in the Louvre.

By 1799, however, he had been ousted from his job with the Commission, and six years later he was forced to give up his rooms in the Louvre when Napoleon decided to turn it into a museum. Fragonard and his wife took lodgings with Marguerite Gérard in the Palais Royal, where he lived, a poor and forgotten figure, until the following year. Fragonard died on 22 August 1806, after eating an ice-cream to cool himself down on his return from a walk in the Champ de Mars.

Mademoiselle Gérard

In 1775 Fragonard's pretty sister-in-law, Marguerite Gérard, came to join the Fragonard household. Under Fragonard's tuition, Marguerite became a highly accomplished artist, painting and exhibiting in her own right. She collaborated with Fragonard on a number of his later works, and may also have been responsible for a change in his style around 1780. Marguerite never adopted Fragonard's rapid brushwork, or his erotic themes. She specialized in quiet domestic scenes, painted with an enamel-like finish and a close attention to detail. Fragonard's works of the 1780s, such as *The Bolt* (pp.130-31), show a similar refinement of handling and the same willowy forms.

Fragonard's pretty sister-in-law
(right) Fragonard probably drew this delicate sketch in 1778, three years after Marguerite arrived in Paris. Unlike her sister, Marguerite was exceptionally pretty, with 'the most lovely black eyes, the most purely oval face and a Roman quality in the contour of her features which invited comparison with a head of Minerva'. Fragonard adored her, and if the couple never actually became lovers, they remained the closest of friends.

Sad Tidings
(left) Under Fragonard, Marguerite first learned to paint in miniature, a technique which strongly influenced her minutely detailed mature painting style. Marguerite's gentle domestic scenes such as Sad Tidings were painted in the new Neo-Classical style, and reflect the fashion, initiated by Jean-Baptiste Greuze, for moralistic pictures which had the power to affect and uplift a predominantly bourgeois audience.

Louvre, Paris

Sparkling Vivacity

Fragonard's art constitutes the final flowering of the Rococo style. His delicate colour and bravura brushwork were ideally suited to the light-hearted erotic themes he chose to paint.

On 30 August 1758, the director of the Ecole de Rome, Charles Natoire, wrote to the Governor of the King's Buildings to report on Fragonard's progress. Fragonard, he said, 'has an astounding ability to change his manner from one moment to the next, and this makes his work uneven'. He further remarked that the young artist had too much impetuosity or *feu* and lacked the patience to make his copies of old masters sufficiently precise.

This remarkable versatility, and Fragonard's natural impatience, are central to an understanding of his painting. They also make him difficult to classify, for he was capable of working in numerous different styles from the brilliant improvisations of the 'fancy portraits' to the meticulous detail and delicate finish of the *Pursuit of Love* (pp.124-5). He also mastered a wide range of subject-matter; apart from his famous erotic pieces he was a superb landscape artist and an excellent portraitist. In addition, he proved himself an imaginative literary illustrator, and provided vigorous drawings for the works of Ariosto and La Fontaine, although these remained unpublished in his lifetime.

'DAZZLING VAGUENESS'

Despite his versatility, however, Fragonard was at his best when working in the rapid, sketchy style of the erotic paintings and the 'fancy portraits'. Although the erotic paintings form only one part of his output it is here that he exploited this style to the best advantage. In paintings such as *The Longed-For Moment* (below) the figures are lightly

The Gardener (c.1750)
(left) This is one of four decorative panels showing scenes from country life. Fragonard's fresh colouring and picturesque treatment of his theme, reveal the influence of his teacher, Boucher.

'Poems of Desire'
(below) Fragonard found a ready market for his 'boudoir' paintings. Their 'decency', wrote the Goncourts, is preserved by the 'lightness of his touch' and by his 'veiled' definition of forms.

Fashionable thrills
(above) This dramatic work of c.1775 shows an elegant boating party in the Rambouillet park. The fantastic landscape, with its swirling waters, emphasizes the lovers' world of make-believe.

Fête at Rambouillet/Gulbenkian Foundation, Lisbon

Giraudon

Louvre, Paris

The Reader (c.1775)
(left) Fragonard's favourite drawing medium was pencil softened by sepia wash. He brushed the ink over wet paper to create a particularly intimate effect. The figures, with their gentle outlines, seem to float over the surface.

Boy Dressed as a Pierrot (after 1785)
(below) Towards the end of his career, Fragonard painted a series of delightful portraits of children. The transparency of his colours and the delicacy of his technique were ideally suited to the depiction of their radiant complexions.

sketched in with a few rapid strokes of the brush. Their bodies are not fully defined, but painted with swift, elusive touches which impart to the picture a suggestive vivacity and animation. It is this quick, elusive style which saves Fragonard's erotic works from being either pornographic or banal. The 19th-century critics Edmond and Jules de Goncourt summed up this feature of Fragonard's work particularly well: 'Every audacity in Fragonard's art . . . trembles, half-hidden beneath the modesty of his handling, that modesty which is expressed in the sketch in which the nude is almost lost to the eye in its shimmer, in which the female form is veiled by a dazzling vagueness.'

SENSUALITY AND WIT

At the same time, this 'dazzling vagueness' heightens the erotic appeal of Fragonard's work. In *The Stolen Shirt*, for example a little cupid pulls the nightgown from a girl whose body is only hazily revealed, as if she were lying behind a fine, gauze curtain, teasing the imagination of the spectator. In *The Longed-For Moment* (left) the rapturous lovers are tantalizingly ill-defined as they merge with the billows of the unmade bed. The brilliant combination of sensuality and modesty, eroticism and wit, turns Fragonard's 'boudoir pictures' into true masterpieces.

Fragonard's creative energy and *brio* found their most novel expression in the so-called 'fancy portraits', two of which he claimed to have painted in an hour. These portraits remain unique in French 18th-century art, and their exact significance is still not fully understood. They are

Wallace Collection, London

Louvre, Paris

Reunion des Musées Nationaux

mostly half-length portraits of men and women, not all of them identified, all in exotic costume, and often with some seemingly allegorical attribute such as a book, or a musical instrument. Their novelty also lies in Fragonard's extraordinary bravura technique. The portraits are painted in a few rough 'shreds' of colour – dashes of thick paint applied with immense speed – which convey the sitters' inner vitality and life. In the painting known as *Inspiration* (p.110), which is probably a portrait of the Abbé de Saint-Non, the dash of Fragonard's handling becomes transformed into the creative energy and tension of the sitter as he pauses in his writings to listen to his Muse.

THE ROCOCO STYLE

Fragonard's art constituted the final flowering of the Rococo style. Originally a fashion in interior decoration, developed between 1710 and 1740, Rococo was formulated partly as a reaction against the sombre architecture and heavy interiors which had been favoured by Louis XIV at Versailles. By contrast, the decorators of the Rococo favoured small, light and elegant rooms enlivened with surface decorations of curves, scrolls and arabesques, interspersed with sketchily drawn figures and floral motifs. The Rococo style of painting and its light-hearted subject-matter were developed to complement this type of decor. Most of Fragonard's works would have been designed for a particular setting, often above the curved frame of a door, and they can only be fully appreciated if they are envisaged in such a setting, placed between mirrors and curved panels.

The Actor
(above and detail right)
Fragonard demonstrated his technical brilliance in a series of 'figures de fantaisie'. He claimed that two of these pictures, including this portrait of the Abbé de Saint-Non in fancy-dress, were painted in just an hour. The paint has been applied with remarkable vigour, in broad strands of colour. As Saint-Non wrote to his brother, 'M. Fragonard is all ardour.'

TRADEMARKS

Dash and Swagger

Fragonard's *feu* – or ardent, impetuous nature – is revealed in his spontaneous brushwork. He worked rapidly and with great panache, loading his brush with pigment.

The Unmade Bed

In the 18th century, the unmade bed was a commonplace of erotic art. For Fragonard, however, it assumed a particular importance and became an integral part of his work. Writing in the 19th century, the Goncourt brothers enthused: 'Merely to touch upon the cambric of the sheets, the creases of the pillow, the indiscretion of the bed curtains, the disorder of the mattress, suffices to intoxicate his Muse.' Fragonard painted the 'tumblings of the counterpane' with obvious delight; his lovers lie enfolded in billowing sheets and drapes, while his playful nudes stretch joyfully among clouds of crumpled silk and winged cupids, their eyes 'still benumbed and heavy with sleep'.

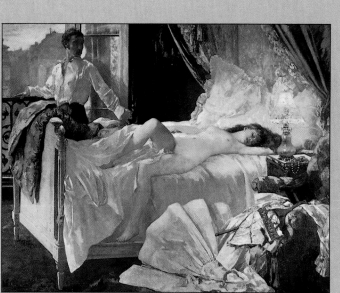

Musée des Beaux-Arts, Bordeaux

Jacquemart André Museum, Paris

Francois Boucher (1703-1770) **Venus Asleep**
(left) Fragonard's teacher, Boucher, made skilful use of the disarrayed couch, especially in his mythological works. In these paintings, a casually spread sheet of rich material is used to enhance the luxury and sensuousness of his nude goddesses.

Henri Rolla (1852-1929) **Gervex**
(above) The subject of this painting – clearly a seduction scene – was taken from a poem by the French writer de Musset. Here the disorder of the bed simply confirms the message conveyed by the woman's hastily abandoned clothes – painted in lurid detail.

The most characteristic exponent of the Rococo style was Fragonard's teacher, Boucher, who was enormously popular with the urban bourgeoisie, then emerging as the new art-buying public. During the Regency of the Duc d'Orleans (1715-23), and the early years of Louis XV's reign, grave financial instability had paved the way for speculators and financiers to make their fortunes. Aristocratic patrons were joined by newly rich businessmen who spent lavishly on works of art to adorn their Paris homes. They were generous, undemanding patrons among whom both Boucher and Fragonard found a congenial market for their art.

Boucher's erotic and pastoral scenes were, for the most part, artificial visions of a pristine countryside peopled with naked nymphs and elegantly dressed 'rustics'. Fragonard's great achievement was to infuse this tradition with a new energy and life, replacing Boucher's idealized goddesses with exuberant, flesh-and-blood figures of women and their lovers engaged in an endless game of amorous hide-and-seek. The same vibrant spirit animates Fragonard's great decorative works such as *The Swing* (p.129), where flickering touches of paint conjure up tiny, graceful figures who enjoy their leisure in a sparkling fantasy landscape.

Bed with Cupids
(right) This is one of Fragonard's most subtle and sensual drawings, executed in pen and ink wash with a touch of watercolour. There is no young girl lying on the fleecy pillows, but the bed's charming disarray and the little brood of cupids leave us in no doubt that this is the setting for love.

Musée des Beaux-Arts, Besançon

THE MAKING OF A MASTERPIECE

The Swing

Fragonard was commissioned to paint *'The Swing'* in 1766 by the Baron de Saint-Julien, a wealthy man who delighted in paintings with titillating themes. The commission had originally been offered to the history painter Doyen, after the Baron had admired one of his religious paintings at the Paris Salon. The Baron was quite explicit in his instructions to the painter. He requested a portrait of his mistress seated on a swing and being pushed by a bishop. 'As for me', he said, 'I should like to appear somewhere in the composition so that I am in a good position to observe the legs of this charming girl.' Doyen indignantly refused the commission and referred the Baron to Fragonard, who happily obliged, only replacing the bishop with a smiling husband.

Fragonard approached the painting with a characteristic blend of frivolity and wit, embellishing the Baron's proposal with a number of delightful details. The excited lap-dog in the foreground, the bemused putti and the Cupid with his finger to his lips add an irresistible humour to the scene. At the same time Fragonard introduces an element of exuberant fantasy. The vast, exotic garden with its misty fountains, summerhouse and lovers embracing in the shadows give the picture a dream-like quality which anticipates the fairy-tale world of the *Fête at Rambouillet (pp.114-15)*.

Wallace Collection, London

Love's indiscretion
(left) Fragonard has shown the young Baron reclining in a bower of flowers and foliage, strategically placed to catch a glimpse of his mistress's legs. His face is lit up with a youthful exuberance which gives his indiscretion a saucy charm.

Doyen's contribution
(right) It was Doyen who suggested the flirtatious detail of 'the lady's slipper flying up into the air'. Fragonard has added a stone Cupid who quietly displays his complicity.

The Baron's Frivolous Tastes

The Baron later purchased another work by Fragonard, entitled *The Useless Resistance* (now lost) – almost identical to this painting – which shows his penchant for erotic themes.

Sainte Geneviève des Ardents
(left) The Baron originally chose Doyen to paint The Swing *on the basis of this religious work.*

> 'Love disguised by a mischievous elegance'
>
> The Goncourts

The Baron's playful proposition
(left) In the Baron's original brief he wanted a bishop to push the swing. This scurrilous suggestion, as Doyen later related, left him confused and speechless, 'particularly in view of the painting (Sainte Geneviève des Ardents*) which had prompted him to make it'. When Fragonard took over the commission he showed an unsuspecting husband happily pushing the swing.*

Gabriel-Francois Doyen/The Church of St Roch, Paris

Reunion des Musées Nationaux

The Useless Resistance/Nationalmuseum, Stockholm

Peter Clark

Gallery

Fragonard's paintings sum up the popular idea of frivolous life in Pre-Revolutionary France. His subjects are almost always light-hearted and often erotic, and they are painted with such verve that it is hard to believe he did not gain as much pleasure from painting them as we do from looking at them. Much of his work deals with love and romance, as

The Gardens of the Villa d'Este, Tivoli *c.1762*
14¾″ × 18¼″ Wallace Collection, London

Fragonard himself made an engraving of this picture in 1763 and it is one of several Italian views he painted soon after he returned to Paris from Italy in 1761. Tivoli was a well-known beauty spot just outside Rome and Fragonard spent much of the summer of 1760 there, making numerous drawings in the company of the Abbé de Saint-Non and his friend, the landscape-painter Hubert Robert.

with The Swing and The Pursuit of Love, and he was a superb painter of female nudes and of the paraphernalia of the boudoir, as in The Bathers and Girl Making her Dog Dance on her Bed.

Fragonard also had a distinctive gift for landscape, and the Villa d'Este at Tivoli seemed to haunt him throughout his life, for its magical atmosphere is evoked in mature works like the Blind Man's Buff.

Late in his career, Fragonard realized that the taste for frothy, titillating themes was passing and in pictures such as A Woman Reading a Book he showed that he could pay tribute to female beauty in a more sober and restrained vein.

The Swing *1766-67* 32½″ × 26″ Wallace Collection, London

This is not only Fragonard's most famous painting, but also one of the most familiar images in 18th-century art. It shows the Baron de Saint-Julien (who commissioned the painting) looking suitably ecstatic as he takes advantage of the view provided by his mistress's uninhibited enjoyment of the swing. The original title was Les Hasards heureux de L'escarpolette (The Happy Hazards of the Swing), *which suggests the light-hearted spirit in which it was conceived. Fragonard never surpassed this painting for delicacy of colour and brushwork, and the figure of the girl, flying through the air with the lightness and beauty of a butterfly, is one of the great triumphs of his art. In 1859 the Louvre had the opportunity to buy this painting, but astonishingly turned it down.*

Scala

The Bathers *c.1765-70*
25½″ × 32″ Louvre, Paris

*Bathing women were popular subjects in 18th-century French art,
whether the figures were representing some mythological story or, as
here, painted for their own sake. Fragonard's handling in this work is
so free and bold that the flesh, draperies and foliage all seem to melt into
the same frothy substance.*

Artothek

Girl Making her Dog Dance on her Bed *c.1765-70*
35″ × 27½″ Alte Pinakothek, Munich

Dogs are often present in boudoir scenes, but usually as a conventional prop rather than as one of Fragonard's 'strokes of delightful immodesty' (The Goncourts). This playful erotic scene is sometimes mistakenly called 'La Gimblette' (the ring biscuit) because in a similar work by Fragonard the woman offers her pet a biscuit.

The Pursuit of Love: Storming the Citadel *1770-72*
125" × 224" Frick Collection, New York

*This and the painting on the opposite page are the first two canvases in
a series of four that Fragonard painted for Madame du Barry, who was
regarded as the most beautiful of Louis XV's mistresses. In 1773 she
returned the paintings to a dismayed Fragonard, probably because his
style was considered out of date in court circles.*

The Pursuit of Love: The Pursuit *1770-72*
125″ × 84½″ Frick Collection, New York

Fragonard's Pursuit of Love *paintings are often considered his masterpieces, but they have had a chequered history. After their rejection by Madame du Barry, Fragonard kept them rolled up in store for years before taking them to Grasse in 1790 and decorating his cousin's house with them.*

The Love Letter *c.1775*
32½″ × 26½″ Metropolitan Museum, New York

*The love letter was a fashionable theme in the 17th and 18th centuries
(perhaps most notably in Dutch painting). The slender figure in this
painting is very different from the chubby and rather doll-like women
Fragonard often depicts, so it may be modelled on a real person. Her
look of slightly furtive anticipation is brilliantly conveyed.*

Woman Reading a Book *c.1775*
32¼″ × 25½″ National Gallery of Art, Washington

This painting makes an instructive comparison with the one on the opposite page, for here the woman reading is demure and studious. In both paintings, however, Fragonard has created beautiful colour harmonies from various yellows and browns highlighted with white, and in both the brushwork is rich and fluent.

Blind Man's Buff *c.1775*
84½" × 77½" National Gallery of Art, Washington

*This and the painting on the opposite page form a pair; indeed, it has
even been suggested that they were originally part of one large single
canvas that was cut up to make two separate paintings. They were
probably painted soon after Fragonard returned from his second visit to
Italy, and the settings are reminiscent of his beloved Villa d'Este.*

The Swing *c.1775*
84½″ × 73¼″ National Gallery of Art, Washington

This picture and Blind Man's Buff *(opposite) were probably painted for Fragonard's patron the Abbé de Saint-Non, but the documentation is inconclusive. The artist has included some charming details, like the young woman looking through a telescope and the laughing couple dangling a little dog in the ornamental pool.*

The Bolt *c.1780*
28¾″ × 36¼″ Louvre, Paris

Late in his career Fragonard adopted a more highly finished style, and here the painting of the various draperies has great polish. A sale catalogue of 1785 describes the picture as follows: 'An interior of a room with a young man and a young woman: the former is bolting the door and the other is trying to stop him; the scene takes place near a bed whose disorder tells the rest of the story clearly enough.' The spotlighting of the figures and the extravagant gestures create a feeling of rather lurid melodrama. Fragonard has chosen a deliberately narrative technique, in the manner of Jean-Baptiste Greuze (1725-1805), to illustrate the woman's imminent surrender. The apple, prominently placed on the bedside table, has even been interpreted as a symbol of the Temptation and Man's subsequent Fall.

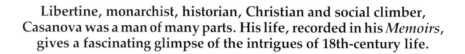

Casanova's Amorous Adventures

Libertine, monarchist, historian, Christian and social climber, Casanova was a man of many parts. His life, recorded in his *Memoirs*, gives a fascinating glimpse of the intrigues of 18th-century life.

Much of Fragonard's art is devoted to the theme of love, not tragic or unrequited love, as is so often the case with works by artists of the following generation, but rather love as a game endlessly pursued to an always satisfying end. Whether such an obsession with sex is a reflection of Fragonard's own personality is doubtful. What it does reflect are the dominant tastes of his patrons, who were mainly exceedingly wealthy, unintellectual and concerned principally with the pursuit of pleasure. One such person was the celebrated dancer Sophie Guimard in whose house, decorated with erotic canvases by Fragonard, were organized weekly orgies in which, according to one contemporary, 'debauchery and vice were carried to the extreme'.

The hedonistic spirit of Fragonard's times is epitomized above all in the life of a man whose very name has come to be used to describe a great lover, Giacomo Casanova. Like Fragonard, Casanova was someone of humble birth who was later to be dependent on the indulgent support of a

Collection Armando Preziosi, Bologna/Robert Harding Picture Library

The ageing roué
(above) The sensual and the scholarly sides to Casanova's nature emerge in Mengs's clever portrait of the elderly libertine, who clutches a learned volume while a rotund cherub flutters by.

The masked ball
(right) The masked ball was a highly popular entertainment. Its promise of intrigue and uninhibited flirtation must have been particularly seductive to Casanova.

Franz Jacob Rousseau/Masked Ball in the Theatre at Bonn/Ministry of Culture for North Rhine-Westphalia, Düsseldorf

Jean-Honoré Fragonard

An unfortunate fiancée
(right) *Manon Balletti was only ten when she first met Casanova, who was a family friend. In her teens she fell passionately in love with him, and by the time she was 17 the couple were engaged. But after years of waiting and pining for her errant fiancée, Manon broke off the engagement – a slight that Casanova never forgot.*

A pious preface
(above) *The sexual exploits recounted in his* Memoirs *earned Casanova his reputation as the world's greatest lover. But in the preface the author declares that he is 'a Christian whose faith is strengthened by philosophy'.*

pleasure-seeking and essentially conservative aristocracy. In contrast to his equally notorious contemporary, the Marquis de Sade, his sexual activities were in no way intended to shock the society in which he moved or to challenge conventional morality. He was, in fact, a social climber, an ardent monarchist, and, in his own way, a devout Christian.

Within these constraints Casanova's life was so filled with intrigues and adventures that it would be barely credible as a novel. It is true that the main source of information about his life is the endearingly egocentric *Memoirs* by Casanova himself; none the less, the evidence of other contemporary documents suggests that though the man might often have embellished his stories, they are fundamentally truthful.

An 18th-century parlour game
(below) *Contraceptive sheaths were an invaluable accessory to debauchery, and provided the popular diversion of balloon-blowing competitions.*

A VERSATILE YOUNG MAN

He was born in Venice in 1725, ostensibly the son of the actor Gaetano Casanova but more probably the result of an affair between Gaetano's actress wife, Zanetta, and the Venetian patrician Michele Grimani. At all events his father died when he was very young, his mother virtually abandoned him, and he was brought up under the unsympathetic guardianship of Michele's brother and Abbé Grimani. From an early age he had to survive through a combination of his wits and influential contacts, and after receiving a degree in law at Padua University, he dabbled in a career first in the Church and then in the army, before, in 1746, becoming a violinist at the Venetian theatre of San Samuele. Two years later he was picked up one night by a Venetian nobleman, Matteo Bragadin, and thereafter embarked on his true career – surviving off the gullibility of the aristocracy. The very night of their first meeting, Bragadin suffered a stroke, and Casanova, realizing the man's belief in the occult, offered to cure him through a consultation of the cabbalistic oracle. By chance the cure worked, thus earning for Casanova Bragadin's undiminishing gratitude and financial support.

Under Bragadin's patronage Casanova could indulge whole-heartedly in an already well-

established life as a philanderer. Initiated at the age of 16 or 17 by two girls in the same bed, his passion for sexual intrigue had soon equalled that of his other two great loves, gambling and eating macaroni. As with many highly promiscuous people, his sexual tastes extended to both women and men. Revealingly, two of his most rewarding affairs of the 1740s were both with actresses who had first appeared to him disguised in men's clothing, the first of whom even going so far as to wear an artificial penis. The second of these actresses, whom he met in 1749 and identified in his diaries as 'Henriette', was perhaps the greatest love of his life, and though when they eventually broke up she scrawled on a window pane the words, *'Tu m'oublieras aussi'* ('You will forget me too'), the memory of her remained with him.

THE RESTLESS TRAVELLER

The restlessness of Casanova as a lover was matched by an incessant need to travel throughout not only Italy but also the rest of Europe. Apart from a possible trip as a teenager to Constantinople and Corfu, his first journey abroad was to Paris in 1750. Here he discovered an impoverished 13-year old girl of Irish descent, one Louise O'Murphy, whose body, when stripped (by him) of both clothes and several layers of dirt, made such an impression on him that he

Longhi/Il Parlatorio

The libidinous Cardinal
(left) The French Ambassador Cardinal de Bernis so enjoyed watching the sexual antics of his mistress and Casanova that he and another nun joined in.

A daring escape
(above) Casanova's revels landed him in prison. He managed to escape by boring a hole in his cell, and climbing onto the roof of the building, from where he nearly fell to his death.

commissioned a German miniaturist to do a painting of it. This work, when sent by Casanova to Louis XV, led to Miss O'Murphy becoming both a mistress of the King and the model for the provocative 'pin-up' by Boucher.

Back in Venice in 1753, by way of Dresden, Prague and Vienna, he soon became involved with another young girl, named 'C.C.' in his *Memoirs*, who was promptly sent off by her irate father to a convent. Her incarceration there did not prevent Casanova from seeing her again, nor did his infatuation with her stop him from falling in love with another nun from the same convent, 'M.M.', who later turned out to be bisexual, and having an affair with both 'C.C.' and the French Ambassador to Venice, the Cardinal de Bernis. This complex situation soon resulted in an orgy involving all four of them, and Casanova being able to indulge in one of his favourite erotic pastimes – eating oysters off the two women's breasts. Eventually, news of these and other sexual doings came to the notice of the Inquisition, and in the summer of 1755 Casanova was thrown into the notorious prison of

Batoni/Albano Cathedral/Robert Harding Picture Library

de Troy/The Garter

Jean-Honoré Fragonard

A fashionable convent
(left) 18th-century Venetian convents were hardly havens of chastity, and Casanova managed to arrange several erotic rendezvous with nuns.

in Florence he was on the point of marrying a girl, who was then revealed to him as an illegitimate daughter of his. In 1774 he was at last given permission to return to his beloved Venice, but after a relatively quiet nine years there, was forced to leave the city again after committing further indiscretions. Finally, in 1785, he was befriended by Count Waldstein and offered a token employment as librarian at the count's castle at Dux in Southern Germany.

Casanova, a man so deeply rooted in the *Ancien Régime*, had the misfortune, like Fragonard, to outlive the French Revolution, the values of which were anathema to him. His last years were sad ones, passed in boredom and relative obscurity at Dux, where he died in 1798, reputedly saying, 'I have lived as a philosopher and die as a Christian'. Though he always had ambitions to be taken seriously as a thinker and indeed when at Dux had published various unreadable books on history and philosophy, his real achievement rests on his *Memoirs*, which had little intention other than to entertain and which remain to this day as fresh and exuberant a record of the 18th century as the art of Fragonard.

The art of titillation
(left) Much of the art and literature of Casanova's time was devoted to describing the thrills of sexual pursuit, from flirtation and initial resistance to final seduction.

Casanova caricatured
(right) Casanova proudly displays the ace of hearts in this contemporary German cartoon, which parodies his ability to win both admiration in bed and money at the gaming table.

Venice's Ducal Palace called the 'Leads'. After 18 months in this damp, rat-infested prison, he managed, with the aid of a spike and quite remarkable ingenuity, to escape to Paris. The story of this escape, told with Casanova's customary verve, made him constantly in demand at the dinner tables of the leading aristocratic families of the time; he was to live off the story for the rest of his life.

From 1757 it becomes as difficult to keep track of Casanova's travels as it does to follow his increasingly complex sexual affairs and other adventures. While gaining his income from the aristocracy, supplemented by unsuccessful attempts at spying and equally thwarted forays into business, he wandered from one place to another, even going as far afield as Moscow and Lisbon. In England he became perhaps the first person to advertise for a woman in a newspaper; in Geneva he managed (according to his own account) to outwit Voltaire; in Berlin he raised a compliment from Frederick the Great; in Spain he was imprisoned for the illegal possession of arms;

Der unter den Namen Space Camino scherzhaft berüchtigte Spieler.

Ik verspiel meine christliche Chevallie all mein Münzerei.

A Year in the Life 1796

By 1796 the worst excesses of the French Revolution were over. France was governed by a five-man Directory which steered a moderate republican course and succeeded in beating off challenges from Right and Left. In March a royalist revolt in the Vendée and Brittany was suppressed, while in May 'Gracchus' Babeuf and his fellow-radical conspirators were arrested before they could launch their intended coup d'état and impose a communistic form of government.

Meanwhile, in the name of 'Liberty, Equality and Fraternity', France found herself at war with most of Europe and had urgent need of capable generals. Hence the meteoric rise of young Napoleon Bonaparte. The Corsican had fast attracted attention in October 1795 by efficiently putting down a rising in Paris with a 'whiff of grapeshot'. Barras, the leading

While Fragonard, a forgotten artist of the Old Régime, eked out a living as a museum curator, the new revolutionary France was making war on the European monarchies. In 1796 the Directory entrusted a young Corsican with his first great command – the invasion of Italy. His name was Napoleon Bonaparte.

Viger/The Temple of Love/Malmaison

Bonaparte in love
(left) This romanticized 19th-century painting of Napoleon and Josephine surrounded by family and friends celebrates a relationship that began in 1795. Napoleon had soon become infatuated with the pretty and well-connected Josephine who regarded the rising young Corsican as an investment for a more stable future. They were married in a civil ceremony in March 1796, the groom leaving to take up his Italian command two days later. His bride, despite his pleas, refused to join him on campaign, preferring the headier and less restrictive delights of Parisian society.

Treaty with Spain
(left) This fan celebrates the signing of the second Treaty of Basle in 1795 which ensured a Franco-Spanish alliance and was followed up the next year by the Treaty of San Ildefonso which secured Spain's active support in the revolutionary cause. This was to the detriment of the British fleet commanded by Admiral Jervis after Spain declared war in October.

Director, had taken Bonaparte under his wing, and the connection was strengthened by Bonaparte's immediate and passionate attachment to Barras' friend and sometime mistress, the lively, pretty Rose de Beauharnais.

NAPOLEON AND JOSEPHINE

Rose was well-known in the society of the Directory period as a leader of fashion but she was also a widow with two children to support. Although not in love with Bonaparte, she was too pragmatic not to see the benefits of marriage to the rising young general. The 26-year-old Corsican and the 32-year-old widow, now renamed Josephine by Bonaparte, were married in a civil ceremony on 9 March. He made use of his older brother's

documents, while Josephine showed the registrar her younger sister's, thus narrowing the gap between their ages.

Napoleon Bonaparte's wedding present from Barras was the command of the French army in Italy against Sardinia and Austria. The General left Paris on 11 March after a two-night honeymoon, and in the following month began the first and perhaps the most brilliant of his many campaigns. Swift victories forced Austria's Piedmontese allies to sue for peace; in May the great victory at Lodi enabled the French to enter Milan and after Bonaparte's triumph at Arcola in November, northern Italy was virtually cleared of Austrian troops, although peace was not made until the following year.

Bonaparte was not yet the emperor and tyrant of later history. In each conquered city he planted a republican 'Tree of

Bonaparte's patron
(left) Barras, as chief member of the five-man Directory, did much to advance Napoleon's career. Impressed with the latter's military expertise, he gave Napoleon command of the Army of Italy in 1796. Barras also introduced the Corsican to his ex-mistress Josephine de Beauharnais.

Johann Fichte
(right) The German philosopher Fichte published his Science of Rights *in 1796. He regarded the individual's right to freedom as the basis of a philosophy that would inspire the Romantic concept of the creative imagination.*

Early champion of communism
(below) 'Gracchus' Babeuf (so named after the Roman tribunes who sought agrarian reform), a political agitator and publisher of Le Tribune du Peuple, *was goaded into action by the appalling economic situation of 1795-6. He founded a 'conspiracy of equals' to overthrow the Directory and to form a state based on collective ownership. The revolt was quashed and Babeuf executed.*

Archiv für Kunst und Geschichte

Giraudon

REPUBLI

Victory at Arcola
(left) Having dealt with Piedmont and Lombardy in the first weeks of his Italian campaign, Napoleon was concerned to drive the Austrians from Mantua and advance on Vienna. His success at Arcola on the second attempt during the three day battle of November 1796 prevented Austrian reinforcements from reaching the city.

New President
(right) John Adams was elected second President of the United States in 1796 after Washington's refusal to accept further nomination.

Bulloz

Archiv für Kunst und Geschichte

Liberty' and encouraged the Italians to shake off their Austrian oppressors. A German visitor to Milan declared that 'From Graz to Bologna people are talking about only one person . . . Bonaparte is a great man, a friend of humanity, a protector of the poor and unfortunate'.

In the midst of this heady atmosphere Bonaparte wrote passionate love letters to Josephine in Paris. She returned perfunctory replies, and having found herself a suitable lover, showed a certain reluctance to join her conqueror-husband.

Elsewhere, the war against Britain, the most implacable of France's enemies, continued. Spain entered the struggle on the side of France, and the British abandoned Napoleon's native island, Corsica, which they had occupied only two years earlier. However, they captured a number of useful West Indian islands, and at Christmas a French attempt to land troops in Ireland was unsuccessful, storms scattering the 14 warships commanded by General Lazare Hoche as they approached Bantry Bay.

Outside Europe, during 1796, there were changes in both Russia and the United States. The lusty and lustful Tsarina, Catherine the Great, died and was succeeded by her son Paul whose mental instability and policy of curbing the nobility made an unlucky combination. He was to be assassinated in 1801. In the USA, the stability of the young American state was demonstrated by the smooth transfer of power from the first president, George Washington, the hero of the Revolutionary War, to his successor John Adams who narrowly defeated his rival Thomas Jefferson in the election.

Nelson in Elba
(left and below) Horatio Nelson had been on active service since war had broken out with revolutionary France in 1793. The British had been forced out of Toulon in 1793 and then Corsica in 1796, so large were the combined navies of France and her new ally Spain. At the end of the year Nelson was ordered to oversee the evacuation of British troops and stores from Elba. The commodore sailed from Gibraltar in the Minerve, arriving at Porto Ferraio in December. The mission was a success and Nelson was to rejoin Admiral Jervis in time to help in defeating the Spanish off Cape St Vincent.

Ill-fated Tsar
(above) On the death of his mother Catherine the Great, in 1796, the rather unprepossessing Paul I became Tsar of Russia. No love had been lost between mother and son, the latter having become somewhat unbalanced at the realization of Catherine's connivance in his father Peter III's murder, which had enabled her to become sole ruler. Paul thus attempted to change anything his mother had done in a reign notable for its frenzied despotism. His reign was only curtailed by his murder five years later.

GALLERY GUIDE

Watteau

The greatest of Watteau's fêtes galantes, his Pilgrimage to the Island of Cythera (pp.26-7) passed into the Louvre after the Revolution. The Louvre also owns the monumental Gilles (p.33) and The Judgement of Paris. There is a fine collection in Berlin, principally displayed in Charlottenburg Castle. Here can be found Watteau's final masterpiece, L'Enseigne de Gersaint (pp.34-5), and also the Rubensian copy of The Pilgrimage to the Island of Cythera (p.23). The Wallace Collection in London owns a selection of the outdoor idylls and La Toilette (p.17), one of his few surviving nudes; Watteau's work can also be found in the National Gallery and at Dulwich. In the States, the Metropolitan Museum, New York, houses Mezzetin (p.32) and French Comic Actors, while the most attractive of the fêtes galantes are in Boston and San Francisco (Fine Arts Museum).

Chardin

The Louvre has examples of all aspects of Chardin's work, from his realistic The Skate (pp.44-5) to the late pastel portraits of himself and his wife. In Stockholm, the National Museum owns several fine genre paintings. Genre works can also be found in Washington (National Gallery of Art) and Ottawa (National Gallery of Canada), which holds The Governess (p.60). Chardin delighted in painting children as in The House of Cards (National Gallery, London) and The Soap Bubbles (Metropolitan Museum of Art, New York).

Boucher

Stockholm has a particularly impressive collection of Boucher's work, of which the finest example is the Triumph of Venus (pp.88-9). Boucher is also well-represented at the Wallace Collection, London. Here, the display is dominated by his depictions of The Rising and The Setting of the Sun (pp.96 and 97), and the museum also owns one of his many portrayals of Mme de Pompadour (p.99), along with a Rape of Europa. The Louvre possesses another version of this latter theme as well as Boucher's Diana after Bathing (p.84). Samples of the artist's work can be found in most major collections in the United States. The Frick houses Boucher's portrait of his wife (p.79), along with a charmingly improbable scene of Winter. The Kimbell Art Museum in Fort Worth has a set of four classical scenes, while the Institute of Arts in Minneapolis contains a rare example of his religious painting. Pictures by Boucher can also be found in Chicago, Los Angeles and Washington.

Fragonard

Fragonard's most famous painting, The Swing (p.121), is in the Wallace Collection, London, which also owns the Fountain of Love and The Gardens of the Villa d'Este, Tivoli (p.120). The Louvre contains the best collection of the artist's work, ranging from the sensuality of The Bolt (pp.130-31) to his most overtly erotic scenes; from the virtuosity of the 'fancy portraits' to his Coresus Sacrificing Himself to Save Callirhoe (p.110). The most playful aspects of Fragonard's style can be seen in his cycle depicting The Pursuit of Love (pp.124 and 125), in the Frick Collection, New York. A fine selection of the painter's work can also be found in Washington, including Woman Reading a Book (p.127) and The Visit to the Nursery (p.111).

BIBLIOGRAPHY

A. Ananoff, L'Opera Completa de Boucher, Rizzoli, Milan, 1980

A. Brookner, Watteau, Colour Library of Art, London, 1967

City Art Gallery, François Boucher, Exhibition Catalogue, Manchester, 1984

P. Conisbee, Painting in Eighteenth Century France, Cornell University Press, Ithaca, 1981

T. E. Crow, Painters and Public Life in Eighteenth Century Paris, Yale University Press, New Haven, 1985

J. Ferré, Watteau (3 volumes), Athena, London, 1972

E. and J. Goncourt, French Eighteenth Century Painters, Cornell University Press, Ithaca, 1981

W. G. Graf and M. Levey, Art and Architecture of the Eighteenth Century in France, Penguin, London, 1972

M. Levey, Rococo to Revolution, Thames & Hudson, London, 1966

D. Posner, Watteau, Cornell University Press, Ithaca, 1983

P. Rosenberg, Chardin, Indiana University Press, Bloomington, 1979

P. Rosenberg, The Franklin D. Murphy Lectures: Chardin – New Thoughts, Helen Foresman Spencer Museum of Art, Kansas, 1983

D. Wakefield, Fragonard, Hippocrene Books, New York, 1977

G. Wildenstein, Chardin, Manesse, Zurich, 1963

M. Wilson, Eighteenth Century French Painting, Phaidon, Oxford, 1979

François-Hubert Drouais (1727-75)

Successful Court portraitist, inheriting the clientele of Nattier. His father, Hubert, was also an artist and Drouais trained briefly under him before completing his studies with Carle van Loo and Boucher. His style was unexceptional but he gained immense popularity for his device of portraying children of the nobility as rather well-groomed beggar boys and rustics. This sentimental perversion of the ideas of Rousseau was a particular feature of the reign of Louis XV. Drouais' best-known work is the full-length portrait of Mme de Pompadour (National Gallery, London), which was begun in 1763 and left unfinished at her death a year later.

Jean-Baptiste Greuze (1725-1805)

French genre painter, specializing in sentimental pictures. Greuze was born at Tournus and studied in Lyon before coming to Paris to make his name. In 1755, he scored a tremendous success at the Salon with his depiction of The Father of the Family Reading from the Bible *(Louvre, Paris) and this ushered in a series of rather mawkish renderings of domestic melodramas. Greuze owed his immense success to the new moral climate, sponsored by Rousseau and Diderot, which sprang up as a reaction against the licentiousness of Boucher and his followers. However, his pretensions to becoming a history painter met with derision and, from 1769, he ceased to exhibit at the Salon. Instead, like Fragonard, he organized private showings of his work at his studio. With the growth of the Neo-Classical movement, Greuze's popularity began to wane, and in response he started to add a prurient edge to his moral*

*allegories (*The Broken Pitcher *in the Louvre, symbolizing a young girl's loss of virginity, is a typical result). Even so, the Revolution ruined him and he died in penury and neglect.*

Nicolas Lancret (1690-1743)

Parisian-born painter, principally remembered for his fêtes galantes. Like Watteau, Lancret was a pupil of Gillot and the slender, puppet-like figures of his early style demonstrate the master's influence. Rapidly, however, he began to imitate the work of his fellow-pupil and his paintings sold well to Watteau's patrons. Lancret was a fine draughtsman and a sensitive colourist, but his pictures have charm rather than poetry. His depiction of the dancer, Mlle Camargo, with members of the Italian Comedy (Wallace Collection, London) is a typically dainty example.

Maurice Quentin de La Tour (1704-88)

The most successful French pastellist of the 18th century. Born in St Quentin, he arrived in Paris as a young man and rapidly decided to exploit the vogue for pastel portraits, which had arisen after the visit of the Venetian artist, Rosalba Carriera, in 1720. His portraits were sharp, vivacious and spiced with wit, and these features brought him commissions at all levels of society. The full-length depiction of Mme de Pompadour (1755, Louvre, Paris) probably caused the greatest stir, but he was also popular with the philosophes, *like Voltaire and Rousseau, who were impressed with his intellect. La Tour had a difficult temperament; he was often rude to his clients, refusing to complete the portraits of patrons who missed a sitting, and in his later years he became somewhat unbalanced.*

François Lemoyne (1688-1737)

Influential history painter, now best-known for being the teacher of Boucher. Lemoyne was born in Paris, the son of a postilion, and received his artistic training from his stepfather, Robert Tournières. His interest was in large-scale allegorical work and, in this field, his major achievement was the immense Apotheosis of Hercules, *which he produced for the Salon de la Paix at Versailles. Lemoyne's style was transitional, blending the verve and sweep of Rubens with more decorative elements that prefigured the Rococo movement. He had a particular talent for female nudes (amply illustrated by* The Bather *in the Hermitage, Leningrad) and communicated this to his pupil, Boucher. Some of their works are remarkably similar, but Lemoyne's untimely death unfortunately precluded any further development in this direction.*

Carle van Loo (1705-65)

The most important member of a family of Franco-Flemish painters. Born in Nice, he trained initially under his brother, Jean-Baptiste, and worked in Rome and

Death in the Louvre

In 1752 Boucher was granted the use of a studio in the Louvre, the Grand Gallery of which is portrayed below in a painting by Hubert Robert. Boucher died in the studio in May 1770, his reputation established.

Hubert Robert: View of the Grande Galerie in the Louvre/Louvre, Paris

Scala

Turin for much of his youth. He was elected to the Academy a year after his return to Paris in 1734 and subsequently enjoyed a career of uninterrupted success. His large-scale decorations and history paintings earned him a reputation that was at least the equal of Boucher's, but which modern critics have found hard to justify. Van Loo's contemporaries thought him rather stupid, but this did not prevent him from winning the highest artistic honours: the post of King's Painter in 1762 and the Directorship of the Academy in 1763.

Charles-Joseph Natoire (1700-77)
Distinguished history painter and academician. Natoire was born in Nîmes and trained in Paris under Lemoyne. Inheriting his master's decorative flair, he gained several important commissions, the most famous being for the Cupid and Psyche *cycle at the Hôtel de Soubise (1737/ 8). Much of his career was spent in Italy, and in 1751 he was appointed Director of the French Academy in Rome. The beauty of the Campagna countryside steered him away from history painting to landscapes and made him very supportive of Fragonard and Robert after their arrival in 1761.*

Jean-Marc Nattier (1685-1766)
Fashionable Court artist in the reign of Louis XV. Nattier began his career as a history painter and his first major commission was for drawings of Rubens' Marie de' Medici *cycle. In 1717 he travelled to Amsterdam, where he painted Peter the Great, and turned increasingly to portraiture after his reappearance in Paris. There, he popularized the taste for depicting ladies of the Court as mythological figures (his Mme Victoire as Diana, in the Louvre, is a splendid example), although his portrait of the neglected queen, Marie Leczinska (Versailles) shows that he was also capable of a noble simplicity. In common with Boucher, Nattier amassed a large collection of shells, which he studied in order to produce the delicate, pearly tones that are the most distinctive feature of his style.*

Jean-Baptiste Oudry (1686-1755)
Influential French painter, specializing in hunting and still-life themes. His father was a picture-dealer and Oudry trained under him and under the portraitist Largillière. The latter recommended him to concentrate on still-life and, in this genre, Oudry fell heir to the tradition of Snyders and Desportes. Louis XV's love of hunting earned him many commissions for paintings of dead game, but Oudry lightened this theme by adding decorative fragments of architecture and baskets of fruit. This approach earned him the directorship of the Beauvais and Gobelins tapestry factories. Here, he employed the young Boucher, who inherited the post after his death. The two men occasionally collaborated – Oudry provided drawings of dogs for Boucher's celebrated Diana after Bathing *(p.84). The completeness of his technique is best exemplified in* The White Duck *(1753, Marchioness of Cholmondeley), where he captured the surface texture of four very different materials, each in shades of white.*

Jean-Baptiste Pater (1695-1736)
Painter of fêtes galantes and Watteau's closest follower. Pater was born in Valenciennes, where he studied briefly

Wallace Collection, London

under Jean-Baptiste Guidé. In c.1713, he travelled to Paris to become Watteau's pupil, but the two men soon quarrelled and Pater returned home. There, he became embroiled in a lengthy legal dispute after refusing to join the local guild, and eventually he was forced to leave Valenciennes. In 1720, he was invited to Nogent, to be reconciled with the dying Watteau and, thereafter, Pater became his closest imitator, specializing in fêtes galantes and picturesque scenes of encampments. His admiration bordered on plagiarism, with groups of figures being lifted directly from Watteau's compositions, but Pater did inject a more overtly erotic flavour that heralded the style of Boucher.*

Hubert Robert (1733-1808)
Notable French landscape painter. Born in Paris, the son of a valet-de-chambre, Robert accompanied the French ambassador to Rome in 1754. There, he gained a place at the French Academy and came under the spell of Panini and Piranesi, both of whom produced romanticized pictures of classical ruins. He made friends with Fragonard, and in 1761 the two men travelled together to southern Italy. Their spontaneous styles, larded with silvery trees and curving balustrades, were very similar. Robert was arrested after the Revolution but escaped the guillotine and became a curator of the Louvre.

Jean-François de Troy (1679-1752)
The son of a noted portrait painter, de Troy studied in Italy until 1706, before returning to France and gaining admission to the Academy. There, his skill at history painting earned him the rivalry of Lemoyne, although it was the latter who gained the title of King's Painter while de Troy only won what was, in effect, the consolation prize of the Directorship of the French Academy in Rome (a post he held from 1738 to 1751). De Troy made his name with his tapestry cartoons and decorative commissions, but is now better known for his genre scenes, which are rather prosaic imitations of the scènes galantes of Watteau and Lancret. The Hunt Breakfast *(1737) in the Wallace Collection is the finest example of this aspect of his work.*

Desportes: Dogs, Dead Game and Fruit
(above) Desportes dominated still-life and animal painting in France when Chardin was embarking on his career. Chardin respected him, and owned two copies of pictures after Desportes.

INDEX